Talents and Distributive Justice

For much of its history, the notion of talent has been associated with the idea of 'careers open to talent'. Its emancipatory promise of upward social mobility has ultimately radically transformed the distribution of advantaged social positions and has had a lasting influence on the very idea of social status itself. Besides its inextricable link with equality of educational opportunity, the notion of talent also came to be associated with some of the most pressing contemporary issues as diverse as the 'war for talent', brain drain, immigration policies, talent management, global meritocracy, the 'excellence gap', the 'ownership' of natural resources, ability taxation, etc.

Nevertheless, while central to egalitarian conceptions of distributive justice, the notion of talent remains to a large extent absent from the voluminous literature on these issues. Unlike concepts traditionally associated with distributive justice, such as fairness, (in)equality, equality of opportunity as well as justice itself, the notion of talent has received only limited examination. This volume brings together a set of contributions discussing some of the most pressing problems and challenges arising out of a reductionist understanding of talents' anatomy, a distorted characterisation of their overall distributive value or talents' non-voluntaristic nature and many other issues revolving around talents, which existing conceptions of distributive justice in education leave either neglected or outrightly ignored.

The chapters in this book were originally published in the journal, *Educational Philosophy and Theory*.

Mitja Sardoč is Senior Research Associate at the Educational Research Institute in Ljubljana (Slovenia). He is author of scholarly articles and editor of a number of journal special issues on citizenship education, multiculturalism, toleration, equality of opportunity, patriotism, radicalisation and violent extremism. He is Managing Editor of *Theory and Research in Education*, Editor-in-Chief of the *Handbook of Patriotism* and *The Palgrave Handbook of Toleration*.

Educational Philosophy and Theory

Series Editor: Peter Roberts, *University of Canterbury, New Zealand*

This series is devoted to cutting-edge scholarship in educational philosophy and theory. Each book in the series focuses on a key theme or thinker and includes essays from a range of contributors. To be published in the series, a book will normally have first appeared as a special issue of *Educational Philosophy and Theory*, one of the premier philosophy of education journals in the world. This provides an assurance for readers of the quality of the work and enhances the visibility of the book in the international philosophy of education community. Books in this series combine creativity with rigour and insight. The series is intended to demonstrate the value of diverse theoretical perspectives in educational discourse, and contributors are invited to draw on literature, art and film as well as traditional philosophical sources in their work. Questions of educational policy and practice will also be addressed. The books published in this series will provide key reference points for subsequent theoretical work by other scholars, and will play a significant role in advancing philosophy of education as a field of study.

Recent Titles

Educational Ills and the (Im)possibility of Utopia
Edited by Joff P. N. Bradley and Gerald Argenton

Design, Education and Pedagogy
Edited by Leon Benade and Mark Jackson

Bildung and Paideia
Philosophical Models of Education
Edited by Marie-Élise Zovko and John Dillon

Bernard Stiegler and the Philosophy of Education
Edited by Joff P. N. Bradley and David Kennedy

Education in Flux
Studies on Time, Forms and Reform
Edited by Mathias Decuypere and Pieter Vanden Broeck

Talents and Distributive Justice
Edited by Mitja Sardoč

For more information about this series, please visit:
www.routledge.com/Educational-Philosophy-and-Theory/book-series/EPT

Talents and Distributive Justice

Edited by
Mitja Sardoč

LONDON AND NEW YORK

First published 2023
by Routledge
4 Park Square, Milton Park, Abingdon, Oxon OX14 4RN

and by Routledge
605 Third Avenue, New York, NY 10158

Routledge is an imprint of the Taylor & Francis Group, an informa business

British Library Cataloguing in Publication Data
A catalogue record for this book is available from the British Library

ISBN13: 978-1-032-34262-7 (hbk)
ISBN13: 978-1-032-34264-1 (pbk)
ISBN13: 978-1-003-32123-1 (ebk)

DOI: 10.4324/9781003321231

Typeset in Myriad Pro
by Newgen Publishing UK

Publisher's Note
The publisher accepts responsibility for any inconsistencies that may have arisen during the conversion of this book from journal articles to book chapters, namely the inclusion of journal terminology.

Disclaimer
Every effort has been made to contact copyright holders for their permission to reprint material in this book. The publishers would be grateful to hear from any copyright holder who is not here acknowledged and will undertake to rectify any errors or omissions in future editions of this book.

Contents

Citation Information

The following chapters were originally published in various issues of the journal *Educational Philosophy and Theory*. When citing this material, please use the original citations and page numbering for each article, as follows:

Chapter 1

Introduction
Mitja Sardoč
Educational Philosophy and Theory, volume 53, issue 8 (2021), pp. 766–767

Chapter 2

Talents and distributive justice: some tensions
Mitja Sardoč and Tomaž Deželan
Educational Philosophy and Theory, volume 53, issue 8 (2021), pp. 768–776

Chapter 3

Two conceptions of talent
Jaime Ahlberg
Educational Philosophy and Theory, volume 53, issue 8 (2021), pp. 777–788

Chapter 4

Against selection: Educational justice and the ascription of talent
Johannes Giesinger
Educational Philosophy and Theory, volume 53, issue 8 (2021), pp. 789–798

Chapter 5

Talents, abilities and educational justice
Kirsten Meyer
Educational Philosophy and Theory, volume 53, issue 8 (2021), pp. 799–809

Chapter 6

Earning rent with your talent: Modern-day inequality rests on the power to define, transfer and institutionalize talent
Jonathan J. B. Mijs
Educational Philosophy and Theory, volume 53, issue 8 (2021), pp. 810–818

Chapter 7

The belief in innate talent and its implications for distributive justice
Mark C. Vopat
Educational Philosophy and Theory, volume 53, issue 8 (2021), pp. 819–832

Chapter 8

A limited defense of talent as a criterion for access to educational opportunities
Winston C. Thompson
Educational Philosophy and Theory, volume 53, issue 8 (2021), pp. 833–845

Chapter 9

China's making and governing of educational subjects as 'talent': A dialogue with Michel Foucault
Weili Zhao
Educational Philosophy and Theory, volume 52, issue 3 (2020), pp. 300–311

Chapter 10

Talents and distributive justice: An interview with Hillel Steiner
Mitja Sardoč
Educational Philosophy and Theory, volume 51, issue 14 (2019), pp. 1393–1398

Notes on Contributors

Jaime Ahlberg is Associate Professor in the Department of Philosophy at the University of Florida. Her main research interests are in ethics, political philosophy and the philosophy of education. She has published on various topics in bioethics, on the ethical and political dimensions of educating children with disabilities, and on the relationship between ideal theories of justice and issues of policy and practice in the nonideal world.

Tomaž Deželan is Professor of Political Science at the Faculty of Social Sciences of the University of Ljubljana and Advisor to the Rector of the University of Ljubljana for quality assurance and development. He is Research Coordinator of the Centre for Social Entrepreneurship at the University of Ljubljana and coordinator of the INOVUP project (Innovative Learning and Teaching for Quality Careers of Graduates and Excellent Higher Education).

Johannes Giesinger is Research Affiliate at the University of Zurich's Centre for Ethics, and he teaches philosophy at the Kantonsschule Sargans (Switzerland). His research interests lie in the philosophy of education and the ethics of childhood.

Kirsten Meyer is Professor of Practical Philosophy at the Humboldt University Berlin. Her research interests are in the philosophy of education, ethics, applied ethics and political philosophy. Her books include "Der Wert der Natur" (*The value of nature* 2003), *Bildung* (2011), and "Was schulden wir kunftigen Generationen" (*What do we owe future generations* 2018).

Jonathan J. B. Mijs' work uses ethnography, experiments and quantitative analysis of survey data to investigate how, in a post-industrial society increasingly driven by inequalities, beliefs in meritocracy are developed and sustained. His interest more broadly is in the interplay between the structural and agentic forces that together shape the course of people's lives. In previous work, he has studied such processes in schools and educational policy, criminal justice and urban social change.

Mitja Sardoč is Senior Research Associate at the Educational Research Institute in Ljubljana (Slovenia) where he is member of the 'Educational Research' research program. He is author of scholarly articles and editor of a number of journal special issues on citizenship education, multiculturalism, toleration, radicalisation and violent extremism, equality of opportunity and patriotism.

Winston C. Thompson is Associate Professor in the Department of Educational Studies at The Ohio State University. Thompson's scholarship focuses upon normative ethical and social/political questions of justice, education, and the public good, with recent efforts analysing dilemmas of educational policy.

Mark C. Vopat is Professor of Philosophy and the Director of the Dr. James Dale Ethics Center at Youngstown State University. He is author of *Children's Rights and Moral Parenting*. His area of specialisation is children's rights. In addition to his work in children's rights, Dr. Vopat has written and presented papers in a variety of areas of applied ethics including: business ethics, engineering ethics, professional ethics, the ethics of boycotting, moral sensitivity, and the intersection of libertarianism and Christianity.

Weili Zhao obtained her Ph.D. in 2015 from the University of Wisconsin-Madison, USA and is currently Assistant Professor in the Department of Curriculum and Instruction at the Chinese University of Hong Kong. With intellectual training in both discourse analysis and curriculum studies, she is interested in unpacking China's current educational thinking and practices at the nexus, and as the (dis)assemblage, of tradition and modernity, East and West.

Introduction

Mitja Sardoč

For much of its history, the notion of talent has been associated with the idea of 'careers open to talent'. Its emancipatory promise of upward social mobility has ultimately radically transformed the distribution of advantaged social positions and has had a lasting influence on the very idea of social status itself. Besides its inextricable link with equality of educational opportunity, the notion of talent came to be associated also with some of the most pressing contemporary issues as diverse as the 'war for talent', brain drain, immigration policies, talent management, global meritocracy, the 'excellence gap', the 'ownership' of natural resources, ability taxation, etc.

Nevertheless, while central to egalitarian conceptions of distributive justice, the notion of talent remains to a large extent absent from the voluminous literature on these (and related) issues. Unlike concepts traditionally associated with distributive justice, e.g. fairness, (in)equality, desert, equality of opportunity as well as justice itself, the notion of talent has received only limited examination. At the same time, several egalitarian scholars started to perceive talents as a form of unfair advantage as holding a particular talent is arbitrary from a moral perspective. On this basis, some proponents of egalitarianism have derived the conclusion that individuals may not deserve the results of the 'lottery of birth' and have equated talents (as a form of 'natural' inequality) with 'social' inequality.

This book, published originally as a journal special issue of *Educational Philosophy and Theory* (volume 53, issue 8) entitled *Talents and Distributive Justice* brings together a set of contributions discussing some of the most pressing problems and challenges arising out of a reductionist understanding of talents' anatomy, a distorted characterization of their overall distributive value or talents' non-voluntaristic nature and many other issues revolving around talents, which existing conceptions of distributive justice in education leave either neglected or outrightly ignored.

The opening contribution to this volume by Mitja Sardoč and Tomaž Deželan identifies some of the problems and challenges arising out of an oversimplified understanding of talents' multifaceted nature and a distorted characterization of their overall distributive value. The introductory part situates the discussion over talents by presenting the 'standard' egalitarian conception of equality of opportunity and the associated idea of fairness embedded in it. The central part aims to elucidate the multifaceted nature of talents and their anatomy. In particular, it advances a dynamic understanding of talents as a hybrid and multifaceted phenomenon. In the final part, they outline two fundamental problems that call into question the cogency of the radical egalitarian conception of educational (in)equality.

In her chapter, Jaime Ahlberg picks up two contrasting conceptions of talent arising out of the literature on social justice. By juxtaposing these two conceptions, she delves into an exegesis of the role of talents in Rawls' *A Theory of Justice*. She concludes her chapter by emphasizing the importance a full theory of talents would have for both education and distributive justice in general.

In his contribution to this volume, Johannes Giesinger identifies two different approaches associated with the notion of talent in relation to questions of distributive justice. In the first section he outlines 'how the justificatory function of talent is seen, in recent liberal debates on distributive educational justice'. The second section of his chapter 'addresses the issue of talent ascription, while the third section spells out the argument against selection'.

Kirsten Meyer kicks off her chapter with a twofold explication of the way talents are being understood in both public and philosophical debates about the justice of school systems as well as the very setup of school systems. The introductory part of her contribution examines in detail the concept of talent and its different key characteristics. She then moves into the direction of framing the discussion over talents as a possible limit to more equality. The concluding parts of her chapter focuses on talents and self-realization as well as the role of school education in opening up possibilities 'and expand pupils' limits as far as possible, instead of justifying alleged limits by attributing a lack of talent'.

In his contribution, Jonathan J. B. Mijs identifies as well as clarifies three non-meritocratic processes associated with talents, i.e. '(1) talent is unequally distributed by the rigged lottery of birth, (2) talent is defined in ways that favor some traits over others, and (3) the market for talent is manipulated to maximally extract advantages by those who have more of it.' His critical examination of the way contemporary conceptions of inequality are being articulated in relation to talents is of particular relevance.

Mark Vopat's chapter questions the prevalent understanding of innate talents and the various theoretical and practical implications this characterization of talents has for discussions over distributive justice.

In his contribution to this volume, Winston C. Thompson critically examines Joseph Fishkin's novel conception of equality of opportunity articulated in detail in his book *Bottlenecks: A New Theory of Equality of Opportunity* and advances 'a limited defense of talent as a criterion for access to developmentally useful educational opportunities'.

Interestingly enough, talents (and human capital in general) have become a leading currency in major contemporary geopolitical transformations. In fact, talents have played a pivotal role in China's central government 'Thousand Talent Program' whose main aim has been to recruit both the 'best and the brightest' foreign researchers as well as to provide an incentive for Chinese scientists living abroad to return home. Drawing upon Foucault's biopower hypothesis and Confucian thought, Weili Zhao's chapter critically evaluates China's making and governing of educational subjects as 'talent'.

The interview with Prof. Hillel Steiner brings to the forefront some of the most pressing conceptual issues over talents and distributive justice. The initial set of questions tackles talents' intricate relationship with phenomena as diverse as the 'war for talent', brain drain, immigration policies, talent management, global meritocracy, the 'excellence gap', the 'ownership' of natural resources, ability taxation etc. The central part of the interview takes up the arguments developed in Prof. Steiner's paper 'Silver Spoons and Golden Genes: Talent Differentials and Distributive Justice'. The concluding question in this interview identifies areas for future research.

This volume is not only a testament both to the complexity of the notion of talent as well as the various educational problems associated with the contemporary conceptions of meritocratic (in)equality but also an open invitation to a further examination of talents and distributive justice.

Talents and distributive justice: some tensions

Mitja Sardoč and Tomaž Deželan

ABSTRACT
For much of its modern history, the notion of talent has been associated with the idea of 'careers open to talent'. Its emancipatory promise of upward social mobility has radically transformed the distribution of advantaged social positions and has had a lasting influence on the very idea of social status itself. Nevertheless, unlike concepts traditionally associated with distributive justice, e.g. fairness, (in)equality, desert, equality of opportunity as well as justice itself, the notion of talent has received only limited examination. This article discusses some of the most pressing problems and challenges arising out of a reductionist understanding of talents' anatomy and a distorted characterization of their overall distributive value. In particular, it aims to address those issues revolving around talents' anatomy existing conceptions of distributive justice leave either neglected or outrightly ignored. The introductory part outlines the basic egalitarian conception of equal opportunities and then proceed with the examination of fairness embedded in it. The central part of the paper identifies the key elements of talents' anatomy. We then discuss some of the implications egalitarianism either leaves out of the discussion or neglects. In particular, we challenge the idea of moral arbitrariness as the key mechanism to discard talents as a form of unfair advantage in the process of competition for advantaged social positions. In the final part, we outline two fundamental problems that call into question the cogency of egalitarian conceptions of talent(s) as a form of unfair advantage.

Talents and distributive justice: some preliminary considerations

For much of its modern history, the notion of talent has been associated with the idea of 'careers open to talent'. Its emancipatory promise of upward social mobility has ultimately radically transformed the distribution of advantaged social positions and has had a lasting influence on the very idea of social status itself. In fact, the idea of 'careers open to talent' has played an important role in both the American and French Revolution representing one of the most important 'innovations' associated with both of them (Carson, 2007). 'The crucial achievement of the two revolutions', as Eric Hobsbawm pointed out in *The Age of Revolution 1789–1848*, 'was that they opened careers to talent' (Hobsbawm, 1996: 189). Article 6 of *The Declaration of the Rights of Man and of the Citizen* emphasises that all citizens are 'being equal in the eyes of the law, are equally eligible to all dignities and to all public positions and occupations, according to their abilities, and without distinction except that of their virtues and talents'. As Rafe Blaufarb emphasizes in his book, *The French Army, 1750-1820: Careers, Talent, Merit*, 'the idea of careers open to talent is one of the most enduring legacies of 1789' (Blaufarb, 2002, p. 2). In fact, 'openness of all positions in society to talent' – as highlighted by S.J.D. Green – has been 'the most radical of the principles of 1789' (Green, 1989, p. 5).

Besides its inextricable link with the abolition of hereditary privilege and equality of opportunity in general, the notion of talent came to be associated also with several of the most pressing contemporary issues as diverse as brain drain (Brock & Blake, 2015), 'war for talent' (Beechler & Woodward, 2009; Michaels et al., 2001), social mobility (Garnett et al., 2008), desert (Sher, 2012), citizenship allocation [e.g. 'Olympic citizenship'] (Shachar, 2011, 2013), migration policy (Cerna & Chou, 2019), the 'ownership' of talents (Goldman, 1987), personal identity (Petrović, 2009), the American Dream (Hauhart, 2016), higher education (Morehouse & Busse, 2014), 'talent spotting' in terrorist recruitment (Bloom, 2017), human resources management (Gallardo-Gallardo & Thunnissen, 2016) neoliberalism (Brown & Tannock, 2009), the 'ownership' of natural resources (Armstrong, 2017), talent management (Lewis & Heckman, 2006), 'ability taxation' (Hasen, 2006; Lockwood et al., 2012; Markovits, 2003; Roemer, 1996 [ch. 6]; Zelenak, 2006), education of the gifted (Merry, 2008) etc.

Given the vast array of areas addressing a particular aspect of talents, the scholarly literature is considerably variegated. At the same time, the spectrum of positions over talents ranges from overly idealistic [and rather naïve] to exceedingly pessimistic. On the one hand, part of the academic as well as the business community champions talents as the next currency of the global meritocracy [ultimately to replace capital]. For example, the notion of talent has played a pivotal role in China's central governement *Thousand Talent Program* whose main aim has been to recruit both the 'best and the brightest' foreign researchers as well as to provide an incentive for Chinese scientists living abroad to return home (e.g. Bentao, 2011; Cao, 2008).[1] Other initiatives aiming to promote the cultivation of talents have mushroomed elsewhere, e.g. the 'Office for Talent' initiative of the British government. Moreover, the idea of talent has been a key policy priority for the OECD in the area of global governance (Tuccio, 2019). Interestingly enough, talents have also become a leading 'currency' in the entertainment industry as TV shows throughout the globe (e.g. *You've got talent, American Idol, Britain's got talent*) have incorporated talent as their central marketing idea (Littler, 2017).

On the other hand, some scholars of a broadly egalitarian orientation, e.g. proponents of radical egalitarianism and the associated idea of radical equality of opportunity (Segall, 2013), view talents as a form of 'unfair advantage'. Given the fact that talents are a morally arbitrary circumstance of one's identity, they have derived the conclusion that individuals may not deserve the results of the 'lottery of birth'. As Harry Brighouse explicates the radical conception of educational equality, 'an individual's prospects for educational achievement should be a function neither of that individual's level of natural talent or social class background but only of the effort she applies to education' (2010: 29). On this interpretation, any outcome in the process of competition for advantaged social positions that are either exclusively or partially the result of talents is therefore questionable as by holding a particular talent, one may be 'unfairly' advantaged. Yet, this bold move in eradicating talents from the meritocratic equation has one important shortcoming: a simplistic and reductionist understanding of talents.

This paper identifies some of the most pressing problems and challenges arising out of an oversimplified understanding of talents' multifaceted nature and a distorted characterization of their overall distributive value. In particular, it aims to address those issues revolving around talents' basic characteristics existing conceptions of distributive justice leave either neglected or outrightly ignored. The introductory part of the paper situates the discussion over talents by presenting the 'standard' egalitarian conception of equality of opportunity and the associated idea of fairness embedded in it. The central part aims to elucidate the multifaceted nature of talents and their anatomy. In particular it aims to advance a dynamic understanding of talents as a hybrid and multifaceted phenomenon. In the final part of this paper, we outline two fundamental problems that call into question the cogency of the radical egalitarian conception of educational (in)equality. Based on the explication of talents' anatomy and the two problems identified as having a considerable impact on our understanding of the relationship between talents and effort, talents should eventually not be rejected as an 'unfair advantage'.

Equality of opportunity and fairness

As a form of 'fair competition among individuals for unequal positions in society' (Fishkin, 1983: 1) and as 'a normative standard for regulating certain types of competition' (Jacobs, 2004: 12), the idea of equal opportunity has a long and venerable history. As James Fishkin emphasizes, equality of opportunity represents 'the central doctrine in modern liberalism for legitimating the distribution of goods in society' (Fishkin, 1983: 1). Part of its on-going charm is undoubtedly linked to its appealing rhetoric and straightforward message. As its advocates argue, equality of opportunity is one of the basic mechanisms for a fair distribution of advantaged social positions. One of its most distinctive characteristics has been a set of [interconnected] commitments associated with fairness, i.e.

[c1] an advantaged social position is to be granted to the best performing person [*the assumption on a meritocracy-based conception of excellence*];
[c2] the distribution of advantaged social positions according to merit is mutually beneficial to both the winner and the loser [*the assumption of mutual advantage*];
[c3] the process of competition for advantaged social positions should only take into account those aspects of an individual's characteristics that are the result of his effort or choices but not those factors which he has no merit or is not responsible for [*the voluntaristic assumption about the nature of the currency of equality*];
[c4] the individual is solely responsible for the outcome of the process of competing for an advantaged social position and the associated change of an opportunity into an advantage [*the assumption of an instrumental nature of transitivity*];
[c5] the rules of competition should be associated exclusively with the performance of tasks associated with the process of competition for advantaged social positions [*the assumption about the excellence of the process of competition for advantaged social positions*];
[c6] the outcome of the process of competition for advantaged social positions is legitimate as far as the process of competition is fair [*the assumption about the fairness of the process of competition for advantaged social positions*];
[c7] differences between individuals that are independent of individuals' choices should be neutralized and the undeserved disadvantages [somehow] compensated for [*the assumption about the unfairness of morally arbitrary circumstances*].

To sum up: (in)equality arising out of the process of competition for advantaged social position is legitimate as long as this process is fair. One of the most important elements of the fairness argument is the voluntaristic assumption about the nature of the currency of equality [c3]. Among the most important aspects distinguishing different conceptions of equality of opportunity is the very nature of what represents an unfair advantage. The egalitarian conception of fairness is based on the distinction between forms of inequality that are beyond an individual's will [involuntary aspect of inequality] and those forms of inequality that are the result of individuals' choices and effort. As Larry Temkin emphasizes, it would be both unjust and unfair, 'when one person is worse off than another through no fault or choice of her own' (Temkin, 1993: 13).

While there are a number of different versions of the fairness argument they all share a common ideal, as Samuel Scheffler argues, what 'inequalities in the advantages that people enjoy are acceptable if they derive from the choices that people have voluntarily made, but that inequalities deriving from unchosen features of people's circumstances are unjust.' (Scheffler, 2003: 5). This idea, as Shlomi Segall points out, is based on the assumption 'that is unfair for one person to be worse off than another due to reasons beyond her control' (Segall, 2008: 10). A basic question that arises here is to determine 'which factors should be counted among people's circumstances and which should be subsumed within the category of choice' (Scheffler, 2005: 6).

That natural differences are undeserved – as Alan Goldman points out – 'means that they should not in themselves be the basis for differential rewards' (Goldman, 1987: 378).[2] As S.J.D. Green emphasizes in his article 'Taking Talents Seriously':

> Individuals do not deserve those gifts because they did not earn them; they are not the product of the effort, or the virtue, or the moral worthiness of those who command them. They are privileges, gratuitously endowed. More important, they are unequally distributed privileges, and the inequality of that distribution is a fundamental and incorrigible cause for the unfairness of the subsequent distribution of resources and welfare between persons in a political community. (Green, 1988: 206–207)

Based on these observations, advocates of radical egalitarianism come to the conclusion that individuals may not deserve the results of 'natural lottery' together with associated benefits [or disadvantages]. 'What seems bad' – as Thomas Nagel emphasizes in *Equality and Partiality* – is not that people should be unequal in advantages or disadvantages generally, but that they should be unequal in the advantages or disadvantages for which they are not responsible (Nagel, 1979, p. 71).

While noble in intent, the radical egalitarian conception of equality of opportunity has problems of its own. One of the most pressing has been its extension of claims for fairness from 'social' to 'natural' factors that might interfere with the process of competition for advantaged social positions and the legitimacy for whatever outcome might occur. The rejection of the meritocratic conception of educational equality and the adoption of its radical alternative is premised on the conception of talents as an unfair advantage. How therefore to square the requirement of fairness embedded in egalitarian conceptions of equality of opportunity with talents' moral arbitrariness. It is this simplistic conception of talents based on the 'lottery of birth' premise that turns out to be a strategic misstep that ultimately hampers the egalitarian claims for fairness. Is there a more elaborated conception of talents?

The anatomy of talents

In one of his well-known essays, 'Prolegomenon to the Principles of Punishment', the prominent British legal philosopher H.L.A. Hart made an insightful comment on punishment, one of the most controversial and pressing public issues in the UK of the 1950s. As he eloquently emphasized, the '[g]eneral interest in the topic of punishment has never been greater than it is at present and I doubt if the public discussion of it has ever been more confused' (Hart, 2008: 1). Contemporary discussions over talents share much the same fate. Part of this straightforward comparison can be associated with the fact that the notion of talent remains to a large extent absent from the voluminous literature on distributive justice [and related issues]. Unlike concepts traditionally associated with this area of scholarly research, e.g. fairness, (in)equality, desert, equality of opportunity as well as justice itself, the notion of talent has received only limited examination leading to a sort of 'conceptual ambiguity' (Robb, 2020: 1).[3] Most interestingly perhaps, as Neven Sesardić emphasizes in his article 'Egalitarianism and Natural Lottery', talents have only recently 'came to be regarded as a political problem' (Sesardic, 1993: 58).

Given the fact that contemporary conceptions of meritocracy rely on an 'essentialized and exclusionary notion of "talent"' (Littler, 2017), this negligence of consideration represents an important omission that comes at a considerable price at the practical, policy and theoretical level. As Lucie Cerna and Meng-Hsuan Chou point out in reviewing the scholarly area of talent management and migration studies literature, 'the lack of conceptual rigor in defining "talent" has real-world implications: it can lead to corrupted practices in internal human resource management, or differentiated policies/packages offered to attract and retain individuals perceived or identified as "talented." (Cerna & Chou, 2019, p. 7). As they emphasise further,

> once a term such as "talent" is loosely defined, this has important consequences for indicator development and measurement. A conceptual looseness can result in diminished purpose of the design process because of the failure to scientifically conceptualize, design, select instruments, and then measure "talent." As a result, the initial ambiguity and plethora of definitions only contribute to further confusion during the policymaking and design processes for talent management programs. (ibid., p. 17)

The elucidation of the notion of talent is therefore of vital importance not only in this area of scholarly research but for discussions on distributive justice more generally. Most importantly, it requires to raise some basic questions that would help to clarify the characteristic features of talents and its relationship with the other key variable that are part of the meritocratic equation, e.g. what are talents' most important [and distinctive] characteristic features? In what way talents differ from effort? What is the relationship between these two variables of the meritocratic equation?

Talents' characteristic features

The first [and perhaps most important] characteristic feature of talents is their non-voluntaristic nature most commonly associated with the idea of moral arbitrariness and the 'lottery of birth'. In contrast to effort an individual may deliberately chose to 'invest' in carrying out a specific task or achieve a particular goal, one's talents are beyond the volitional power of individuals' holding them. Talents, as George Sher emphasizes in his article 'Talents and Choices' – designate 'any unchosen ability that has an impact on how well or badly its possessor is capable of performing any task' (Sher, 2012, p. 16). On this interpretation, talents are largely [or even exclusively] the result of factors that are beyond an individual's control. In fact, no individual can influence which talents one is supposed to possess [and to what extent].

The second characteristic feature associated with talents is their unequal distribution. It is most likely that no two individuals would possess similar or equal talents [or to the same degree]. In fact, any equalization of talents would have as an effect that they would cease to function as an advantage. As Steven R. Smith emphasizes, 'talents (however they are conceived substantially) are qualities or characteristics that can only be talents if not everyone possesses them to the same degree' (Smith, 2001, p. 28). Differences in individuals' 'natural' abilities [including talents] are therefore a condition of their social desirability. Actually, an equal distribution of talents among individuals would undermine their overall distributive value as well as function as a possible source of envy between the untalented and the talented [or vice versa] (Christofidis, 2004; Dworkin, 1981). Unlike goods whose equal distribution would have positive effects, the unequal distribution of talents is a fundamental condition for their socially desired status and distributive value.

The third characteristic feature talents share in common is their social status. As Alan Goldman emphasizes, what counts as a talent ultimately 'depends on social demand at a time for the use of a particular ability or characteristic' (Goldman, 1987, p. 392). What qualifies as a talent in a given socio-historical circumstance is actually dependent on a variety of different factors. For example, a talent's social status is to a large extent dependent on how widely a particular characteristic might be available at a given point in time. The inequality of talents, as Douglas Rae points out, '*is not a phenomenon of nature, but a phenomenon of nature as mediated and reified by human culture*. Nature creates a wide variety of human capacities; culture picks out certain of those capabilities to treat as relevant or important' (Rae, 1983, p. 70 [author's emphasis]). Talents are therefore not temporally fixed dispositions: what qualifies as a talent in this day and age may not qualify as a talent in another period of time or under other circumstances. What ultimately qualifies as a talent is therefore a socio-historical contingency.

The fourth characteristic feature of talents is their nontransferability. In contrast to individuals' transferable resources that may be sold, borrowed, inherited or otherwise transferred, talents [like individuals' other nontransferable characteristics, e.g. handicaps] are both nontransferable and nonalienable (Roemer, 1996, p. 123). This distributive limitation has important implications for the overall perception of talents and has been viewed as one of its characteristic features that raises a range of separate questions. It is due to their nontransferability that talents cannot qualify – at least on a radical egalitarian conception – as a legitimate currency of equality.

Moreover, a talent's overall value – in contrast to factors such as higher socio-economic status that enables individuals a direct advantage compared to those from a lower socio-economic position – lay in its potential. The advantage a particular talent provides to an individual is therefore not direct, but conditional. As Hillel Steiner emphasizes, '*talents are labour products*: their creation and development requires the application of gestational, nutritional, medical, educational and training services' (Sardoč, 2019, p. 1394 [emphasis in the original]).

Furthermore, another important feature to be emphasized is talents' interconnection with effort. While the 'standard' understanding of the relationship between talents and effort views the two variables as distinct entities, there are scholars emphasizing that their relationship is far more complex and dynamic. As Alain Trannoy points out, a talent is a 'cumulative variable' comprising 'past-effort, current effort and innate talent' (Trannoy, 2019, p. 1). At the same time, this relationship between the two variables that are part of the meritocratic conception of educational equality is not a fixed one. A talent, as Trannoy argues, is present in its 'purest' form at the beginning of one's life and over time becomes blurred with effort (2019, p. 2).

There is another important differentiating characteristic between talent and effort that needs to be pointed out. Effort is a type of variable that depends [each time] on an individual's performance, whereas a talent represents a constant variable or a permanent potential advantage in the set of individuals 'natural' abilities. As Alain Trannoy emphasizes, '[t]alent is different from luck because the latter is occasional, while talent is recurrent' (2019, p. 5).

To sum up: talents' characteristic features explicated above provide a considerably more complex [and puzzling] picture compared to some of the main characterizations in the existing scholarly literature on equality of opportunity. [4] In contrast to the 'standard' view that uses a simplified and reductionist understanding, talents are neither natural, inborn or fixed [at least in the traditional understanding]. The elaboration of talents as a 'hybrid' and 'fluid' variable explicated above has important repercussions for our understanding of the requirements of fairness associated with equality of opportunity [in particular the radical egalitarian alternative]. In fact, this shift towards a 'hybrid' and 'fluid' conception of talent leads to major conceptual repercussions associated with distributive justice. As Rawls emphasizes in *A Theory of Justice*

> The extent to which natural capacities develop and reach fruition is affected by all kinds of social conditions and class attitudes. Even the willingness to make an effort, to try, and so to be deserving in the ordinary sense is itself dependent upon happy family and social circumstances. It is impossible in practice to secure equal chances of achievement and culture for those similarly endowed, and therefore we may want to adopt a principle which recognizes this fact and also mitigates the arbitrary effects of the natural lottery itself. (Rawls, 1971, p. 74).

Conclusion: the triangulation of talent

Acknowledging talents' multifaceted nature and its complex anatomy leaves scholars of a broadly egalitarian orientation with a set of problems as it undermines one of the most important distinctions associated with fairness and social justice in general, i.e. the distinction between 'just' and 'unjust' inequality. While the rejection of the meritocratic conception of educational equality and the adoption of its radical egalitarian alternative would have important implications for social policy, there are important conceptual issues that are in need of further elucidation. Despite the fact that the meritocratic conception of educational equality is neither ideal nor optimal, the elimination of talents from the equation would actually open several other problems while allegedly solving one. Its reliance on a simplistic conception of talents actually turns out to be a strategic misstep that ultimately hampers its [otherwise legitimate] claims for fairness.

In particular, two problems challenge the cogency of radical equality of opportunity and radical egalitarianism in general, i.e. [*i*] the delimitation problem and [*ii*] the disconnection problem. On the one hand, the key challenge associated with the 'delimitation problem' lays in setting out criteria that would enable us to determine whether a particular element influencing the process of competition for advantaged social positions is either part of chance or that of choice. This distinction, as George Sher argues in his book *Equality for Inegalitarians*, enables us 'to make the cut between just and unjust inequalities' (Sher, 2011, p. 2–3). On the other hand, the disconnection problem challenges the very relationship between 'natural' and 'social' inequality and its basic assumption that 'natural inequalities are caused by differences in natural resources, while social inequalities are caused by differences in social resources' (Lewens, 2010, p. 270).

Without providing conclusive evidence to these two problems, egalitarianism [at least its radical alternative] looses much (if not all) of its intuitive appeal. As Neven Sesardić emphasizes,

> It is ironical that contemporary egalitarians find differences in talents so embarrassing if we recall that, historically, egalitarians themselves demanded the removal of all impediments to the full expression of different natural abilities. So, one of the pillars of the eighteenth century egalitarianism was the thought that persons are entitled to the fruits of the exercise of their personal capacities and talents. (Sesardić, 1993, p. 58).

Conceiving talents primarily as a form of unfair advantage therefore remains trapped in the relation best described by Thomas Nagel in his article 'Justice and Nature' 'between natural unfairness and social injustice' (Nagel, 1997, p. 304). As he points out, '[t]he more one regards nature as a given, the less one will regard society as accountable for those inequalities in whose generation nature plays a central role' (Nagel, 1997, p. 305).[5] The basic question is therefore not how to square the requirement of fairness embedded in egalitarian conceptions of equal opportunity with talents' moral arbitrariness but how to ensure that the 'race' for advantaged social positions is fair and inequalities that are the result of a process of competition legitimate as equality of opportunity and inequality are not mutually exclusive.

Notes

1. For a critical analysis of China's 'governance' of talent and its genealogy, see Zhao (2020). A detailed presentation of China's 'multi-layered talent schemes' including sponsors & targeted talent is elaborated on page 6 of this article.
2. The distinction between 'social' and 'natural' forms of inequality is a complex and problematic one so it cannot be adequately addressed in this article (e.g. Lewens, 2010). For a discussion of justice and nature, see Nagel (1997).
3. A rare exception to this trend include Christman (2015), Dworkin (1981), Steiner (2002), Green (1988), Merry (2008), Meyer (2014), Robb (2020), Roemer (1996), Sadurski (1990), Sesardić (1993), Sher (2012) and Trannoy (2019).
4. The list of talents' characteristic features explicated in this section does not claim to be exhaustive. For an explication of talents' characteristic features present in talent management and migration studies literature., see Cerna and Chou (2019).
5. For a critical examination of Nagel's article 'Justice and Nature', see de los Santos Menéndez (2020).

Disclosure statement

No potential conflict of interest was reported by the authors.

References

Armstrong, C. (2017). *Justice and natural resources: An egalitarian theory*. Oxford University Press.
Beechler, S., & Woodward, I. (2009). The global 'war for talent. *Journal of International Management, 15*(3), 273–285. https://doi.org/10.1016/j.intman.2009.01.002
Bentao, Y. (2011). Internationalization at Home. *Chinese Education & Society, 44*(5), 84–96. https://doi.org/10.2753/CED1061-1932440507
Blaufarb, R. (2002). *The French Army, 1750–1820: Careers, Talent, Merit*. Manchester University Press.
Bloom, M. (2017). Constructing expertise: Terrorist recruitment and "talent spotting" in the PIRA, Al Qaeda, and ISIS. *Studies in Conflict & Terrorism, 40*(7), 603–623. https://doi.org/10.1080/1057610X.2016.1237219
Brock, G., & Blake, M. (2015). *Debating brain drain: May governments restrict emigration*. Oxford University Press.
Brown, P., & Tannock, S. (2009). Education, meritocracy and the global war for talent. *Journal of Education Policy, 24*(4), 377–392. https://doi.org/10.1080/02680930802669938
Cao, C. (2008). China's brain drain at the high end. *Asian Population Studies, 4*(3), 331–345. https://doi.org/10.1080/17441730802496532
Carson, J. (2007). *The measure of merit: Talents, intelligence, and inequality in the French and American Republics, 1750–1940*. Princeton University Press.
Cerna, L., & Chou, M. H. (2019). Defining "talent": Insights from management and migration literatures for policy design. *Policy Studies Journal, 47*(3), 819–848. https://doi.org/10.1111/psj.12294
Christman, J. (2015). Our talents, our histories, ourselves: Nozick on the original position argument. In: T. Hinton (ed.), *The original position* (pp. 77–96). Cambridge University Press.
Christofidis, M. C. (2004). Talent, slavery and envy in Dworkin's equality of resources. utilitas, *16*(3), 267–287. https://doi.org/10.1017/S0953820804001177
de los Santos Menéndez, F. (2020). Naturally and socially caused inequalities: Is the distinction relevant for assessments of justice? *Res Publica*, 1–15. https://link.springer.com/article/10.1007/s11158-020-09469-x
Dworkin, R. (1981). What is equality? Part 2: Equality of resources. *Philosophy & Public Affairs, 10*(4), 283–345.
Fishkin, J. (1983). *Justice, equal opportunity, and the family*. Yale University Press.
Gallardo-Gallardo, E., & Thunnissen, M. (2016). Standing on the shoulders of giants? A critical review of empirical talent management research. *Employee Relations, 38*(1), 31–56. https://doi.org/10.1108/ER-10-2015-0194
Garnett, B., Guppy, N., & Veenstra, G. (2008). https://doi.org/10.1111/j.1573-7861.2007.00049.x
Goldman, A. H. (1987). Real people (natural differences and the scope of justice). *Canadian Journal of Philosophy, 17*(2), 377–394. https://doi.org/10.1080/00455091.1987.10716442
Green, S. J. D. (1988). Taking talents seriously. *Critical Review, 2*(2-3), 202–219. https://doi.org/10.1080/08913818808459533
Green, S. J. D. (1989). Emile durkheim on human talents and two traditions of social justice. *The British Journal of Sociology, 40*(1), 97–117. https://doi.org/10.2307/590292
Hasen, D. M. (2006). Liberalism and ability taxation. *Texas Law Review, 85*(5), 1059–1113.
Hauhart, R. C. (2016). *Seeking the American dream: A sociological inquiry*. Palgrave Macmillan.
Hobsbawm, E. (1996). *The age of revolution 1789–1848*. Vintage Books.

Lewis, R. E., & Heckman, R. J. (2006). Talent management: A critical review. *Human Resource Management Review*, *16*(2), 139–154. https://doi.org/10.1016/j.hrmr.2006.03.001

Lewens, T. (2010). What are 'Natural Inequalities? *The Philosophical Quarterly*, *60*(239), 264–285. https://doi.org/10.1111/j.1467-9213.2009.621.x

Littler, J. (2017). *Against Meritocracy: Culture, Power and Myths of Mobility*. Routledge.

Lockwood, B. B., Nathanson, C. G., Weyl, E. G. (2012). Taxation and the allocation of talent http://home.uchicago.edu/weyl/ taxationandthe allocationoftalent.pdf

Markovits, D. (2003). How much redistribution should there be? The *Yale Law Journal*, *112*(8), 2291–2329. https://doi.org/10.2307/3657477

Merry, M. (2008). Educational justice and the gifted. *Theory and Research in Education*, *6*(1), 47–70. https://doi.org/10.1177/1477878507086730

Meyer, K. (2014). Educational justice and talent advancement. In V, K. Meyer (ed.), *Education, justice and the common good* (pp. 133–150). Routledge.

Michaels, E., Handfield-Jones, H., & Axelrod, B. (2001). *The war for talent*. Harvard Business School Press.

Morehouse, C., & Busse, M. (2014). *How to keep a competitive edge in the talent game: Lessons for the EU from China and the US*. Centre for European Policy Studies.

Nagel, T. (1979). *Mortal questions*. Cambridge University Press.

Nagel, T. (1997). Justice and nature. *Oxford Journal of Legal Studies*, *17*(2), 303–321. https://doi.org/10.1093/ojls/17.2.303

Petrović, N. (2009). Equality of opportunity and personal identity. *Acta Analytica*, *24*(2), 97–111. https://doi.org/10.1007/s12136-009-0046-4

Rae, D. W. (1983). *Equalities*. Harvard University Press.

Rawls, J. (1971). *A theory of justice*. Harvard University Press.

Robb, C. M. (2020). Talent dispositionalism. *Synthese*, 1–18.

Roemer, J. (1996). *Egalitarian perspectives: Essays in philosophical economics*. Cambridge University Press.

Sadurski, W. (1990). Natural and social lottery, and concepts of the self. *Law and Philosophy*, *9*(2), 157–175. https://doi.org/10.2307/3504581

Sardoč, M. (2019). Talents and distributive justice: An interview with Hillel Steiner. *Educational Philosophy and Theory*, *51*(14), 1393–1398.

Scheffler, S. (2003). What is Egalitarianism? *Philosophy Public Affairs*, *31*(1), 5–39. https://doi.org/10.1111/j.1088-4963.2003.00005.x

Scheffler, S. (2005). Choice, circumstance, and the value of equality?. *Politics, Philosophy and Economics*, *4*(1), 5–28. https://doi.org/10.1177/1470594X05049434

Segall, S. (2008). *Health, luck and justice*. Princeton University Press.

Segall, S. (2013). *Equality and opportunity*. Oxford University Press.

Sesardić, N. (1993). Egalitarianism and natural lottery. *Public Affairs Quarterly*, *7*(1), 57–69.

Shachar, A. (2011). Picking winners: Olympic citizenship and the global race for talent. *The Yale Law Journal*, *120*(8), 2088–2139.

Shachar, A. (2013). Talent matters: Immigration policy-setting as a competitive scramble among jurisdictions. In: T. Triadafilopoulos (ed.), *Wanted and welcome? Policies for highly skilled immigrants in comparative perspective* (pp. 85–104). Springer.

Sher, G. (2011). *Equality for inegalitarians*. Cambridge University Press.

Sher, G. (2012). Talents and choices. Noûs, *46*(3), 400–417. https://doi.org/10.1111/j.1468-0068.2010.00790.x

Smith, S. R. (2001). The social construction of talent: A defence of justice as reciprocity. *Journal of Political Philosophy*, *9*(1), 19–37. https://doi.org/10.1111/1467-9760.00116

Steiner, H. (2002). Silver spoons and golden genes. In D. Archard in C. Macleod (eds.), *The moral and political status of children* (pp. 183–194). Oxford University Press.

Temkin, L. S. (1993). *Inequality*. Oxford University Press.

Trannoy, A. (2019). Talent, equality of opportunity and optimal non-linear income tax. *The Journal of Economic Inequality*, *17*(1), 5–28. https://doi.org/10.1007/s10888-019-09409-7

Tuccio, M. (2019). Measuring and assessing talent attractiveness in OECD countries [OECD Social, Employment and Migration Working Papers No. 229]. OECD: Paris.

Zelenak, L. (2006). Taxing endowment. *Duke Law Review*, *55*(6), 1145–1181.

Zhao, W. (2020). China's making and governing of educational subjects as 'talent': A dialogue with Michel Foucault. *Educational Philosophy and Theory*, *52*(3), 300–311. https://doi.org/10.1080/00131857.2019.1646640

Two conceptions of talent

Jaime Ahlberg

ABSTRACT
In the liberal egalitarian literature, the concept of talent is inflected according to its use in broader arguments surrounding the nature of justice. In particular, sometimes talent is understood as a desirable inborn property, while at other times it is understood as a matter of inhabiting a favorable social position. Rawls's arguments in A Theory of Justice provide useful expressions of these two very different conceptions of talent and their relationship to justice, and much of this paper involves an exploration of those arguments. The former sense of talent informs Rawls's fair equality of opportunity principle: those with equivalent levels of talent and effort are to face similar prospects. According to the latter, what is significant about talent is not its innate origins, but rather its enabling the possession of desirable goods. This second sense of talent is implicit in Rawls's difference principle: though it is arbitrary that the talented have the ability to command high wages, it is nonetheless fair to keep those wages because the worst off benefit most from that arrangement. In this paper I explore how the two conceptions of talent operate in these influential arguments, with the broader aims of clarifying the nature of talent and its relevance to social justice.

In the liberal egalitarian literature, the concept of talent is often inflected according to its use in broader arguments surrounding the nature of justice.[1] Sometimes, talent is understood as something akin to a desirable inborn property ('golden genes' in Nagel's words (1997)), while at other times it is understood as a matter of inhabiting a favorable social position. The former sense of talent informs the familiar Rawlsian idea of fair equality of opportunity: those with equivalent levels of talent and effort are to face similar life prospects. The justification here is that it would be an affront to one's moral nature to be barred from valuable opportunities simply because of social factors outside of one's control. According to the latter sense of talent however, what is significant about talent is not its innate origins, but rather that possessing it enables one to achieve desirable goods. On this understanding, the talented are those who can garner high wages and vary their productivity according to how much they are paid. To be 'talented' or 'untalented' hinges on whether one's traits and abilities are socially appreciated. This conception of talent is integral to Rawls's argument for the difference principle, for, though it might be a matter of chance that the talented have the ability to command high wages, it can nonetheless be fair that they keep those wages because the worst off (i.e. the 'untalented') prefer that arrangement relative to alternatives.

The primary aims of this paper are to identify these two conceptions of talent, and to explore how they are implicated in Rawls's influential principles of justice. I focus on Rawls for two reasons. First, his arguments in *A Theory of Justice*, particularly those surrounding the fair equality of opportunity and difference principles, provide useful expression of these two very different conceptions of talent.[2] His framework is thus useful for illuminating them. Further, Rawls's impact on political philosophy in the past half century has shaped how many political philosophers think about, and invoke, the concept of talent in their arguments. Unpacking what Rawls has to say has the potential to shed light on how the concept of talent is being used in other areas of the literature. For these reasons, his framework is a useful and fruitful place to begin.

1. The sources of talent and justice's purview

Rawls uses 'natural endowment' and 'natural asset' as equivalent to 'talent' in many places in *A Theory of Justice*. Natural endowments are taken to be the physiological and psychological hands one is dealt at birth, and greater endowments are taken to indicate the presence of talent. A favorable hand is usually taken to include traits like mathematical, musical, or artistic aptitude; physical strength or agility; and personality traits correlated with social or economic success (ambitiousness, or charisma, for instance). Possessing high IQ often acts as a paradigm example of having a talent. It is considered to be a fixed part of one's natural constitution, and correlated with achievement and success. Having a high-level IQ is sometimes described as being 'gifted' by nature.

I suspect this understanding of talent reflects the commonsense view: a talent is an inborn cause of success. It is thus distinguishable from other potential causes of success, including the effort we dedicate to our activities, the ways our social background might advantage us, or the mere luck we might occasionally enjoy. Whether we have talent, on this view, is thus not fully under anyone's control.[3] No amount of our own will and determination, or others' efforts to elicit it, can generate talent in us if it was not already latent within us. On this view we would say that Ludwig Wittgenstein, for example, was simply born with a cognitive apparatus that enabled him to make analytical and imaginative leaps most other people's brains cannot. And similarly, Michael Phelps simply has a bodily constitution that enables him to swim faster than almost anyone else, most of the time. These are perhaps truly exceptional cases of talented individuals, but the point generalizes: there are many ways in which native potentials can enable success. Talented coders have minds that are suited to computational logic, talented surgeons have remarkably steady hands, talented painters have a keen eye, and so on.

A moment's reflection on this view reveals, however, that this conceptualization of talent cannot be the whole story. The successes of Wittgenstein, Phelps, and others who are deemed talented, while certainly dependent upon the deployment of physical and mental powers, are not solely a matter of individual, internal constitution. Social factors mediate and enable inborn potential in many ways. First, ability has to be developed through training and education. Wittgenstein could not have written the *Tractatus* had he not been educated to be literate, and Phelps could not have become an Olympic athlete without years of physical conditioning. To borrow Hillel Steiner's phrase, in this sense talents are 'labor products'.[4] A full array of social supports enable the cultivation of inborn potential, from the production of food and housing to the provision of high quality education and specialized training.

Furthermore, social attitudes and practices assign value to characteristics and abilities, thereby encouraging some and inhibiting others. In this way, social factors determine whether inborn potentials are even developed, and if so, how they are expressed. Rawls is sensitive to this insight:

> [N]ative endowments of various kinds (say, native intelligence and natural ability) are not fixed natural assets with a constant capacity. They are merely potential and cannot come to fruition apart from social conditions. Educated and trained abilities are always a selection, and a small selection at that, from a wide range of possibilities that might have been fulfilled. (2001, pp. 56–57; also see 1971, 74)

Second, the activities toward which native potentials are directed must be considered socially valuable in order for developed capacities to qualify as talents. A person who can display the physical movements made possible by double-jointedness is not thereby talented, even if she possesses a rare ability. Perhaps there is some small entertainment value to performing such movements, but even if so, that value is not explained or justified by its role in social cooperation. The movements of double-jointedness are neither a source of, and nor are they implicated in, social or economic goods or practices. Infrastructure is not in place to capitalize off of someone exercising such movements, or to cultivate such movements in people who are double-jointed. Being double-jointed does not figure into the central narratives of people's plans of life.[5] Conversely, social approval and regard made possible the academic history, community, and institutions that enabled Wittgenstein to pursue his intellectual endeavors. Society has supported intellectual research enough to make it possible for people to organize their lives around academic pursuits. In the case of Phelps, society enabled the presence of swimming pools, sports equipment and trainers, and competitions throughout his childhood, which were all precursors to his Olympic performances. Our society is captivated by such displays of physical excellence and competition. It devotes enormous resources to cultivating and providing occasion to exhibit these physical feats, making the career of 'championship swimmer' a meaningful life path.

It is important to underscore the extent to which talent is not simply a matter of excellent natural aptitude. In the particular cases of Wittgenstein and Phelps, while their unique abilities are associated with exceptional performance, they are also associated with what some would identify as disability or impairment. Some observe that Wittgenstein's lifestyle and documented behaviors, including the content and style of his philosophical writings, meet the criteria for Autism Spectrum Disorder (ASD).[6] A similar story can be told about Phelps. He has an unusually long arm span and large feet, hypermobile joints, a below normal range of lactic acid, and a lanky body-type ('marfanoid habitus'), the latter of which puts him at increased risk of cardiac failure.[7] The bodily features that position Phelps to be a champion swimmer are also associated with below average bodily functioning and unusual structure.[8] As Bickenbach has argued, 'the impairment continuum overlaps (or is coincident with) the talent continuum' (2009, p. 121). It would be a mistake to say that a singular, superior and natural property grounds only success, in these cases.

These observations do not show that in cases of talent, there is *no* inborn source of success. They show, instead, that the success cannot be fully attributed to natural endowment. The presence of talent is at least partly a matter of social practices and human choices, beyond what nature delivers. Talent is thus best understood as an interrelationship of natural, personal, and social causes; it cannot be reduced to either one of these causes. Nor is it constituted by the 'sum' of such causes, because it develops as the body and environment interact with each other. Put more strongly, there is no such entity as a body that exists outside of its environment such that we could 'add' the two together; there is only ever body-in-environment.[9] Only when natural endowments are interpreted via social context and developed through individual and social effort over time—usually through educational provision—can they amount to 'talents'. An important consequence is that talents are not merely natural resources that can be harvested for the social good, since they cannot exist independently of the social environment itself. Neither are they merely labor products.

The fact that talents are not merely natural resources is significant because, at least for contractualist arguments like Rawls's, social responses to the facts of nature fall under justice's purview. For contractualists, distributive justice does not hold society accountable for mitigating 'natural inequalities', simply because justice is a fundamentally *social* matter. As Rawls put it:

> The natural distribution is neither just nor unjust; nor is it unjust that persons are born into society at some particular position. These are simply natural facts. What is just and unjust is the way that institutions deal with these facts. (1971, 102)

Social institutions are non-arbitrary patterns of human action, capable of being changed according to human will. Social response to the natural distribution is thus subject to the demands of justice. What is to be determined is exactly how society ought to respond to the arbitrariness of the natural distribution.

Rawls writes at multiple points that social contingencies and natural chance are equally arbitrary from the moral point of view (e.g. 1971, p. 75; 2001, p. 75). And yet, his theory treats these two sources of arbitrariness in one's life differently.[10] Talent, insofar as it is *native* potential, is a legitimate determinant of one's access to socially valuable opportunities. But, insofar as one does not *deserve* one's talents, Rawls also argues that it is *not* a legitimate determinant of one's access to income and wealth. Only the ability to benefit the least advantaged can legitimate access to additional income and wealth.

In the next two sections I further explore how talent figures in Rawls's arguments in these two different ways. First, I consider that view that talent is native potential that legitimates access to socially valuable opportunities. Second, I consider the alternative that talent is the possession of social leverage, whereby the talented are simply those who can vary their productivity in response to incentives.

2. Talent as native potential

Rawls leans on a naturalistic understanding of talent in his arguments regarding how to distribute socially valuable opportunities, including educational and labor market opportunities. He argues that that access to such opportunities should not be determined by one's social background, but rather by one's natural aptitude (i.e. talent) and one's willingness to learn. According to the fair equality of opportunity principle:

> [A]ssuming that there is a distribution of natural assets, those who are the same level of talent and ability, and have the same willingness to use them, should have the same prospects of success regardless of their initial place in the social system, that is, irrespective of the income class into which they were born. (1971, 73)

Talent, ability, and effort are here taken as factors that are legitimate determinants of one's access to socially valuable opportunities. In this regard they stand in stark contrast to other possible determinants of opportunity: most significantly for Rawls, social class status, but also factors like family and religious background, race, and gender. While the fact that one possesses native potential is a matter of pure chance, it is nevertheless a salient consideration with respect to the social opportunities to which one should have access under fair equality of opportunity.

Talent-possession is relevant to the availability of social opportunity for a few reasons, in Rawls's view. First, native ability is relevant to the particular tasks a person can perform, and thus to the shape that one's cooperation in social endeavors can take. Wittgenstein and Phelps were suited to the particular activities that made them famous in part because of their natural constitutions. And presumably, each would have been ill-suited to the activities of the other.

Second, social opportunities are essential to the plans of life that can realize each person's good. In the latter chapters of *Theory,* Rawls argues that human beings enjoy realizing their native and developed capacities, and that this enjoyment increases the more complex the capacities that are involved. This is his so-called Aristotelean Principle of human motivation (1971, p. 426). While Rawls refrains from specifying any particular activities or conceptions of the good as desirable regulative ideals, he does claim that human beings have a 'relatively strong and not easily counterbalanced' tendency to want to train and mature their innate potentials. The plans of life that contribute to human beings' flourishing will thus be those that provide outlets for such development and expression 'in significant measure' (1971, p. 428). Educational endeavors and meaningful work are critical locations for sharpening one's attention on, and devotion to, capacity growth.[11] Educational and employment prospects should thus be fairly available to those who have the natural proclivities and will to make use of them.

Third, providing opportunities for people to develop their native potentials is good for everyone. Each member gets to enjoy the fruits of others' capacity development, and observing others improve and express their capacities inspires in people a desire to develop their own capacities.[12] Moreover, since no one person can develop all sides of her nature, participation in society makes it possible to experience of a wide range of human potentialities that would otherwise be unavailable. This is a great good for each member, but also a great good for all. In one of Rawls's more stirring passages, he exploits the metaphor of a symphony orchestra to emphasize that it is only through a social union based on the capacities of all that each can enjoy the full fruits of characteristically human activity:

> As a pure case to illustrate this notion of social union, we may consider a group of musicians every one of whom could have trained himself to play equally well as the others any instrument in the orchestra, but who each have by a kind of tacit agreement set out to perfect their skills on the one they have chosen so as to realize the powers of all in their joint performances. [...]
>
> [P]ersons need one another since it is only in active cooperation with others that one's powers reach fruition. Only in a social union is the individual complete. (1971, pp. 524–525)

It is through social cooperation that each person's inborn potential can be harnessed and transformed into a distinctive, wholly actualized form of human fulfillment.

Through this picture of human motivation, and with an understanding of the unique goods made available through social cooperation, we can begin to interpret Rawls's arguments much earlier in *Theory* defending the fair equality of opportunity principle. There, he claims that those from disadvantaged social backgrounds who are barred from valuable opportunities can justifiably complain 'because they were debarred from experiencing the realization of self which comes with a skillful and devoted exercise of social duties. They would be deprived of one of the main forms of human good' (1971, p. 84). Fair equality of opportunity protects meaningful engagement in the social activities to which one is suited. In doing so, it protects the ability of each individual to formulate and act upon rational plans of life that promote the cultivation of native capacities. The incisive, energetic inner-city kid suffers a special kind of injustice when she is effectively excluded from lucrative, interesting, and prestigious careers because she lacks access to a fancy educational background and exclusive, powerful social networks. Not only is she barred from the wealth and privilege such a path would produce, but more significantly, she is prevented from experiencing the 'realization of self' that is attendant upon developing her mental and social agility toward the valuable ends made possible only by collective activity (1971, p. 84).[13] What's more, a robust sense of one's worth is deeply reliant upon self-realization and engagement in socially valuable ends. Given these stakes, Rawls argues that socially valuable opportunities are to be equally distributed: opportunities to secure socially valuable positions should track comparative talent and effort levels.[14] An unequal distribution of these opportunities would express unequal regard for individuals' living fully human lives. This would amount to a form of disrespect; it would be an assault on human dignity.

It is not an accident that 'talent' is construed in naturalistic terms in the context of these arguments for equality of opportunity. Native potentials are relevant to the activities that will in fact facilitate a person's development, and they are relevant to the shape of the contribution one can make to the joint social product. On this line of thinking, the native potential one brings to the world grounds one's entitlement to socially valuable opportunities. Of course, one does not *deserve* one's talents, and so one is not entitled to more social opportunity *because* one's talents merit it. Rather, justice demands that people be afforded the environment necessary to flourish as human beings, which necessarily involves self-development and growth.[15]

The real world implications of this view of talent are perhaps clearest in the domain of education.[16] In Section 1, I hope to have aroused suspicion regarding the view that there are such things as superior natural endowments per se, because social inputs are always required to spur and shape the exercise of natural potential. Nevertheless, fair equality of opportunity does not require us to provide a valence to the natural potentialities in question. Justice does not demand that we justify, for example, the (additional) resources necessary to support 'gifted and talented' programs on the ground that *being talented* merits them. Rather, under this principle, the rationale for providing educational goods to 'gifted and talented' children is the same rationale for delivering educational goods to any child: doing so is necessary to provide an education that will enable the formation of and participation in a rational life plan.[17] A parallel argument would need to be given in order to justify (additional) resources in cases of disability. Failing to provide this type of education for any child constitutes a form of neglect. If gifted and talented programs uniquely provide educational resources adequate to this purpose for a group of children, then we have a *prima facie* case for the provision of gifted and talented programs. Of course, in our world, there is reason to doubt that labeling children as gifted tracks anything about their native endowment, rather their privileged social background (Merry, 2008, p. 56). But surely there are exceptional cases in which students' natural constitutions are not well-matched to standard educational environments, in the sense that those environments are insufficient to deliver educational goods that will connect children to life paths that will be good for them. This will happen to any student who is an outlier with respect to the standard educational system. In such cases, for the development of capacities implicated in the ends of rational life plans, gifted programing is not only justified, but *prima facie* required.

3. Talent as the possession of social leverage

In the previous section I argued that the nature of a person's native potential is relevant to what is the most rational plan of life for her, in her circumstances. The particular opportunities that are valuable in achieving each person's good, by living a rational life plan, will thus vary according to human natural difference (among other contingencies). This is why talent (construed as natural endowment) is a non-arbitrary, legitimate basis upon which to distribute social opportunity.

One might resist linking native endowment to access to all socially valuable goods, however, and on Rawlsian grounds. After all, while natural endowment is relevant to the particular *social opportunities* that would figure into a rational plan of life, natural endowment is not relevant to the value of *income and wealth*. Income and wealth really are all-purpose goods in a way that particular social opportunities are not; any individual can use income and wealth to pursue their plan of life. Since everyone has a claim to pursue her conception of the good, everyone has an equal claim to the maximum amount of income and wealth possible, regardless of native endowment. Those with more native potential are not deserving of more resources, in virtue of that potential.

Nevertheless, Rawls famously points out that an unequal distribution of income and wealth can benefit the least well off more than an equal one. In certain cases, an unequal distribution can increase the total amount of income and wealth available: when those who are able to command high wages in exchange for their labor are allowed to keep more material rewards for that labor (i.e. they are incentivized), they will produce more. In such circumstances the social product is augmented, and some of this additional labor product can be distributed to the least well off. It is under these conditions that income and wealth inequality is consistent with justice. Indeed, inequality might be required, insofar as it constitutes the circumstances that are to the greatest benefit of the least advantaged. It is not, then, in virtue of possessing native potential that people are entitled to a greater share of income and wealth, but rather in virtue of being well-placed to augment social wealth that one can become entitled to a greater share. Characterizing the nature of this arrangement, Rawls writes:

> [T]he difference principle represents, in effect, an agreement to regard the distribution of natural talents as a common asset [...]. Those who have been favored by nature, whoever they are, may gain from their good fortune only on terms that improve the situation of those who have lost out. The naturally advantaged are not to gain merely because they are more gifted [...]. (Rawls, 1971, p. 101)

Despite the language Rawls uses here, what is important about talent in these arguments is not its natural origins. Rather, what is significant is whether people are well-positioned to be productive and are susceptible to incentives. If someone is so positioned, then she qualifies as talented.[18] Of course, one explanation for why someone is so positioned is that she embodies native potentials that, with social investment, can greatly contribute to the social product. Perhaps a person is born with the potential to become extremely clever or imaginative, or strong or dexterous, in ways that are in high demand. But another possibility is that one is favored by social factors. Having a loving upbringing, excellent education, and strong community of support may well enable exceptional aptitude and productivity, even for those with average native potentials. On this view, there is no 'natural baseline' according to which a person is talented. Rather, to be talented is a matter of possessing social leverage: one can choose, or not, to deploy socially-valued abilities in order to improve the circumstances of the least advantaged. Talents are thus deeply contextualized, and though necessary, native potential is neither sufficient nor the morally salient feature of talent.

This understanding of talent evades several of the problems faced by the naturalistic conception. First, a bright line between the natural and social causes of talent need not be drawn; all that is relevant is the ability to command more rewards than others are able to command. This avoids the conceptual problem of diagnosing the point at which a (natural) potential becomes a (developed) talent. It also avoids the major practical problem of identifying who has socially valuable, natural proclivities. No one thinks that we currently have a foolproof (or even relatively decent) system for identifying native potential. Diagnostics and monitoring are marred by a poor understanding of human physiology and cognition, as well as well documented biases like racism, sexism, and classism (Merry, 2008). Native potential is also sometimes obscured by countervailing factors. For many years deafness was falsely taken to be evidence of diminished cognitive capacity, for instance. Poor nutrition, a troubled home life, or an environment of disaffected peers can inhibit the development and expression of native potential. Practical obstacles infuse the possibility of implementing an accurate system whereby the 'truly' natively endowed are distinguished from those who are not so endowed, such that each is fairly afforded, say, the educational provisions that will align children with fitting social opportunities.[19]

Second, this view avoids the misleading classification of people as simply 'talented' or 'untalented' in virtue of their inborn potentials. As the Wittgenstein and Phelps examples illustrate, people have a number of characteristics, some of which are socially valued or otherwise conducive to living well, and some of which are not. One or another of one's natural qualities might suit one to fulfill this function, while the same, or other, qualities might make it difficult to do so. (Perhaps this was the case with Wittgenstein.) Further, over time, a person can shift in and out of having the relevant kind of social leverage, developing the skills and capacities that will facilitate leverage, not developing them, or letting them atrophy. Emphasizing the social and personal causes, valuations, and uses of talent, tames the false impression that nature is an all-powerful determinant of opportunity.

Some might object to my interpretation of Rawls, and claim that the conception of talent as the possession of social leverage cannot be so easily divorced from the naturalistic conception. Text surrounding the argument for the difference principle sometimes suggests that it is natural potential alone that distinguishes those who can be more productive from those who cannot. For example: 'If [improving the long-term expectation of the least favored] is attained by giving more attention to *the better endowed*, it is permissible; otherwise not' (1971, p. 101, emphasis added). Indeed, a standard reading of Rawls's principles is that, while fair equality of opportunity addresses the accidents of social fortune, the difference principle addresses the accidents of natural fortune, so that the two principles together neutralize all forms of morally arbitrary (dis)advantage (Kymlicka, 2001; Pogge, 1989). On this reading, the central point of the difference principle is to capitalize on the natural gifts of the talented, for the benefit of those who are less favored by nature. If this interpretation is correct, then perhaps there is only one sense of talent after all: the naturalistic one.

I acknowledge that the difference principle requires that we capitalize on natural differences, when doing so is to the greatest benefit of the least advantaged. And, most of the time, Rawls *does* refer to the talented as those who are 'better endowed' or 'favored by nature'. However, the textual evidence is mixed. Consider these passages:

> In designing institutions [people] undertake to avail themselves of the accidents of nature *and social circumstance* only when doing so is for the common benefit. [...]
>
> No one deserves his greater natural capacity *nor merits a more favorable starting place in society*. But it does not follow that one should eliminate *these* distinctions. There is another way to deal with *them*. The basic structure can be arranged so that *these* contingencies work for the good of the least fortunate. Thus we are led to the difference principle if we wish to set up the social system so that no one gains or loses from his arbitrary place in the distribution of natural assets *or his initial position in society* without giving or receiving compensating advantages in return. (1971, 102 emphases added; see also 15)

More important than a textual interpretation of *Theory*, however, is the point that the *cause* of the talented's productive capacity is immaterial to difference-principle reasoning. As long as the liberty principle and fair equality of opportunity are satisfied, then *for whatever reason* the talented are able to produce more, they are permitted to keep extra rewards for their efforts so long as doing so is to the greatest benefit of the least advantaged. This inequality is acceptable to the least advantaged because they are better off than they would otherwise be. And, it is acceptable to the better off. They agree to the constraint on their earning power because they realize they are absolutely reliant on the cooperative scheme for their good opportunities (which scheme would not be possible without the buy-in of all), and they realize the difference principle makes it reasonable for the less well-off to agree to cooperate (1971, p. 103).

What are the real world implications of this conception of talent? If we return to the domain of education, making use of this conception of talent looks problematic. Especially when children are young, whether they are talented in this sense is indeterminate, as they are not yet in a position to withhold their productivity for material incentives. Perhaps with older children it is different, as the likelihood that they will possess the relevant kind of social leverage comes into view. Already by the ages of seven or eight (sometimes earlier), aptitude and interest in socially valued activities like literary interpretation and mathematics, sports, public speaking, and musical and artistic performance, are visible. In such cases, the difference principle might provide a reason to develop the strengths of these children, for the benefit of all.[20]

Still, I am skeptical that highlighting children's capacity for high future productivity, and presumably their corresponding ability to withhold that productivity for greater profits (i.e. talent), amounts to a good reason for extra educational provision. First, even at young ages, the privileges associated with a favorable upbringing are enormously significant to the development and expression of inborn potential. To focus on inchoate capacities for future productivity is likely to compromise the opportunities of children who have not had the benefit of a good upbringing. Doing so risks inhibiting these children's conceptions of what is possible for themselves, and more broadly jeopardizes their formations of their preferred life plans. In such a system social fortune would very easily come to dictate children's life prospects from a young age. Educational programs grounded in arguments based on the promise of talented children to grow the social product threaten to compound the benefits of social privilege that is unevenly distributed at birth. In our world, we have seen gifted and talented programs disproportionately populated by students of wealthy parents who are able to purchase tutoring and additional testing (Merry, 2008), and confer cultural enrichment and training in how to behave in socially desirable ways (Lareau, 2011).

Second, and more fundamentally, when the difference principle is applied to adults deciding to vary their productivity in response to market incentives, it is operating in a context in which reasonable and rational moral agents decide for themselves which life paths they want to pursue. They can decide to withhold their productivity if they like, or not. As Rawls put it, free and equal persons 'agree to regard' their productive capacities as a common asset. Children are not in a parallel position to hold their productivity hostage for more resources, or indeed to consent to their productive capacities being regarded as communal goods. They are not yet moral agents, and not yet participants in the kind of social reciprocity modeled by the difference principle. Their capacities to reciprocate, as well as their disposition to reciprocate and to view themselves as participants in a social project broader than themselves, are still forming. Children are potential reciprocators. But as such, they are not yet party to the kind of social relationship the difference principle relies upon for its justification. Whatever the value of difference principle reasoning to thinking about economic justice between adults, it does not straightforwardly address justice in the context of children. We still need an account of why, and to what extent, children's potential productive capacities are to be harnessed for benefit of all.

4. Conclusion

I began this paper by attempting to destabilize the common view that talent is simply an inborn cause of success. Social factors shape and mediate the expression of native potential to enable achievement and success. But how do natural and social forces come together to inform a plausible concept of talent, and in what ways is talent relevant to us and to our relationship with society? I've looked to Rawls to begin exploring these questions, because of his influence on our collective conversation about distributive justice and because his principles of justice invoke both natural and social understandings of talent.

I have argued that Rawlsian fair equality of opportunity relies on a conception of talent as native endowment, because native endowment is relevant to the socially valuable opportunities that will facilitate both a person's development and her contribution to social cooperation. The 'talented' and 'untalented' have a symmetrical claim to some package of opportunities that will enable acting on a suitable life plan. Insofar as they would need different packages of opportunities in order to live out suitable life plans, the talented and untalented would have a claim to different packages. I have also argued that Rawls's difference principle instead construes talent as the possession of a certain kind of social leverage. The difference principle relies on a characterization of the talented as those who can choose, or not, to be socially productive, in response to the incentives of income and wealth. The 'talented' and 'untalented' have asymmetrical claims; only the talented have a justice-based claim to additional income and wealth, so long as the provision of that extra income and wealth ultimately redounds to the benefit of the least advantaged.

Unfortunately, Rawls never defines talent, and neither of Rawls's principles is explicitly sensitive to the ways in which talent is an interrelationship of natural, personal, and social causes. Nor do his principles appear unified on how talent should be construed. This is perhaps unsurprising, as fair equality of opportunity and the difference principle are distinct normative principles guided by different values, and with different aims and distribuenda. And yet, thinking about Rawls's assumptions about talent has been instructive. In particular, it has helped to reveal the relevance of native potential to social justice: namely, that our native potential can be harnessed to contribute to the unique form of human fulfillment that is social cooperation, which benefits not just ourselves but everyone involved. It also offers an interpretation of the positional nature of talent: being talented is (at least partly) a matter of occupying a more desirable position than others in some respect. As my brief remarks about the context of education suggest, instances in which we must decide whether, or how, to offer social support to shape native potential are particularly challenging to theorize. In such cases what is at stake is not merely what people are owed in terms of social resources, but who they will become as people. A full theory of talent would recognize the importance of these many considerations.

Notes

1. Important liberal egalitarian work that implicates the concept of talent in discussions of justice includes: Brian Barry (2005) *Why Social Justice Matters.* Malden, MA: Polity Press; Ronald Dworkin (2000) *Sovereign Virtue: The Theory and Practice of Equality.* Cambridge: Harvard University Press; Martha Nussbaum (2006) *Frontiers of Justice: Disability, Nationality, Species Membership.* Cambridge, MA: Harvard University Press. Other relevant work includes: Anita Silvers and Leslie Pickering Francis. (2005). Justice through Trust: Disability and the 'Outlier Problem' in Social Contract Theory. *Ethics 116*, 40–76; Steven R. Smith. (2001). The Social Construction of Talent: A Defense of Justice as Reciprocity. *Journal of Political Philosophy 9*, 19–37.
2. Most of my analysis is confined to the original edition of *A Theory of Justice* and surrounding literature, simply because the two conceptions of talent—as natural, and as social—clearly appear there, and because his later arguments complicate the way talent figures in his theory (see footnote 14 for elaboration).
3. Of course, developments in gene editing technology may introduce opportunities for prospective parents to shape the native potentials of their offspring. In such cases it may well turn out that *someone* is responsible for native potential, so far as the causal power of DNA goes. It is worth noting, however, that it cannot turn out that we are responsible for *our own* native potential. Regardless, I hold gene editing to the side here, because I take it that a central reason such genetic intervention is controversial is precisely that it injects human agency into processes that have hitherto been happenstance (Sandel, 2007). Here, I am interested in how the native potentials that arise by chance figure into social justice arguments. Cases involving human intervention would necessitate different kinds of considerations.
4. See interview with Steiner in Sardoc, M. (2019). See also Steiner (2002).
5. In the next section I will discuss Rawls's Aristotelean Principle, and its role in characterizing the kinds of activities that make for a good human life, given humanity's natural characteristics. While Rawls does acknowledge that people can organize their lives around plans that are apparently trivial and non-social (this is his case of the grass-counter, 1971, p. 432), he does not think that these kind of activities make for characteristically human lives (1971, p. 433).
6. Fitzgerald (2000). Of course, personal agency can be relevant to how, and even whether, ASD and other disorders manifest. Smith (2005) has persuasively argued that the characters of those who are disabled are integral to the extent of the misfortunes they suffer; some respond more fruitfully to their circumstances than others. Personal agency is thus relevant to one's identification as disabled (by oneself and others) as well as to talent-possession related to disability status. While this paper focuses on two conceptions of talent—natural and social—personal agency is also relevant to this discussion and a full theory of talent would account for it.
7. The case of Michael Phelps is detailed and helpfully discussed in Barnes (2016, pp. 14–15).
8. I do not mean to imply a fully naturalistic (i.e. non-normative) account of disease or disability. Here, I only mean to say that a particular description of the body (e.g. including the presence of ASD or marfinoid habitus) can be associated with either positive or negative wellbeing, because the body acts within, and is acted upon by, social context. See Barnes (2016).
9. Thank you to an anonymous reviewer for encouraging me to think about this point further, and for suggesting some language.
10. It is worth pointing out that Rawls's claim that natural and social inequalities are equally arbitrary from the moral point of view occur early in *Theory* (Chapter 2), where he is only presenting an intuitive argument in favor of fair equality of opportunity and the difference principle, together understood as 'Democratic Equality'. Later (in Chapter 3), when Rawls gives his explicitly contractualist defense of Democratic Equality, he emphasizes the different ways in which social and natural inequalities are relevant to each principle. For a helpful discussion of the role of the arbitrariness argument in Rawls, see Shiffrin (2010, pp. 118–34). Also consider G. A. Cohen's understanding: 'a cause of inequality is "morally arbitrary" if it does not justify that inequality because of the kind of cause of inequality it is' (1995, p. 161). 'Moral arbitrariness' here is not equivalent to 'a matter of chance', or 'independent of human agency'. Rather, one must establish whether a cause is morally arbitrary with respect to a target concept or principle. See also Nozick (1974, p. 227).
11. Some native potentials do not require much, or even any, educational resources to develop, and are not socially rewarded. Bickenbach (2009) proposes that perfect pitch is like this: one simply has it or not, and though it may be intrinsically valuable, it is not particularly instrumental for securing social rewards. I agree that perfect pitch does not need to be cultivated, but in my view it is not right to say that it is not part of any socially valuable activity. Perfect pitch is part of musical excellence, which is widely considered to be socially valuable. Abilities that are not regarded as socially valuable are not best construed as talents, as the double-jointedness example illustrates.
12. Rawls calls this inspired desire the Aristotelean Principle's companion effect (1971, p. 428).
13. While Rawls seems to be thinking specifically of social and political 'offices' in this passage, I would suggest that we can apply these claims to educational opportunities as well. First, fair equality of opportunity is to govern the distribution of 'powers and opportunities' and 'prospects of culture and achievement', in which educational positions and opportunities very plausibly figure. Second, the remarks Rawls makes about

education at various points in the original version of *Theory* support the interpretation that he viewed educational goods in this manner. He writes, for instance, that 'the value of education should not be assessed solely in terms of economic efficiency and social welfare. Equally if not more important is the role of education in enabling a person to enjoy the culture of his society and to take part in its affairs, and in this way to provide for each individual a secure sense of his own worth' (1971, p. 101).

14. Clayton (2001) argues that Rawls is not entitled to this kind of argument given his political liberalism, because it assumes a particular conception of wellbeing: one that privileges self-realization. Reasonable people can disagree about whether wellbeing includes self-realization. Importantly, Clayton uses this critique to mount the broader argument that Rawls cannot make a principled distinction between social and natural sources of human difference. Each, Clayton claims, is as morally arbitrary as the other, and must therefore be governed by justice in the same way. I want to point out two senses of talent in Rawls: one that is primarily naturalistic (relevant to fair equality of opportunity), and the other that is about social positioning (relevant to the difference principle). If Clayton is right, then 'talent' may not be differently inflected once the arguments of political liberalism are operative, since Rawls cannot argue that natural endowment is salient to self-actualization. My investigation is largely internal to *Theory*, where the two senses of talent are most clear and where Rawls's political liberalism plays less of a role. I thus set Clayton's argument aside, as I am less interested in unifying Rawls's body of work than in a close examination of the natural and social conceptions of talent that Rawls's early work helps to illuminate.
15. Merry (2008) has argued in favor of 'gifted and talented' education on the grounds that gifted children are entitled to an education that adequately challenges them, for this is essential to human flourishing. Notably, he argues that fair equality of opportunity cannot itself act as a justification for additional resources to develop and provide gifted and talented education. This is because, he argues, opportunities cannot be afforded on the basis of morally arbitrary factors. I have tried to show that, when it comes to social opportunities, natural talent is *not* a morally arbitrary factor. Of course, it is still a matter of luck, or chance, that one is talented, but to be a matter or luck or chance is only one way to be morally arbitrary. See note 10 above.
16. For two different educational analogs to the fair equality of opportunity principle, see Swift (2003) and Brighouse and Swift (2008).
17. Nagel (1997, p. 316) claims that this sort of rationale stretches the concept of equality too far because 'it is pretty clear that the good of education is unequally distributed in such a system'. I disagree. The *value* of education would be equally distributed (according to its connection with individual flourishing), even if educational resources had to be unequally distributed in order to achieve that end.
18. Cohen (1997) employs the same conception of talent, eschewing the conception of talent as native potential.
19. Satz (2007) characterizes this observation as a serious objection to the meritocratic principles of educational equality, some of which were identified in footnote 16.
20. Rawls articulates the educational entitlements of the talented in even stronger terms: 'The difference principle would allocate resources in education, say, so as to improve the long-term expectation on the least favored. If this end is attained by giving more attention to the better endowed, it is permissible; otherwise not' (1971, p. 101). In this passage, implications of the difference principle are drawn under the naturalistic sense of talent, which invites familiar problems: the conceptual difficulties in distinguishing 'primarily natural' causes, and the practical problems in distinguishing native potentials from social fortunes. This view is also subject to the two concerns I raise next, regarding the appropriateness of difference-principle reasoning in the context of children and their education.

Acknowledgments

Thank you to Jonathan Rick, Harry Brighouse, and an anonymous referee for helpful discussion on the main ideas in this paper. I'd also like to thank Center for Humanities and the Public Sphere at the University of Florida for sponsoring a writing retreat in the spring of 2019, at which a draft of this paper was completed.

Disclosure statement

No potential conflict of interest was reported by the author(s).

References

Barnes, E. (2016). *The minority body*. Oxford: Oxford University Press.

Bickenbach, J. (2009). Disability, non-talent and distributive justice. In K. Kristiansen, S. Vehmas, & T. Shakespeare (Eds.), *Arguing about disability* (pp. 105–123). New York, NY: Routledge.

Brighouse, H., & Swift, A. (2008). Putting educational equality in its place. *Education Finance and Policy, 3*(4), 444–466. https://doi.org/10.1162/edfp.2008.3.4.444

Clayton, M. (2001). Rawls and natural aristocracy. *Canadian Journal of Philosophy, 1*(3), 239–259.

Cohen, G. A. (1995). The Pareto argument for inequality. *Social Philosophy and Policy, 12*(1), 160–185. https://doi.org/10.1017/S026505250000460X

Cohen, G. A. (1997). Where the action is: On the site of distributive justice. *Philosophy Public Affairs, 26*(1), 3–30. https://doi.org/10.1111/j.1088-4963.1997.tb00048.x

Fitzgerald, M. (2000). Did Ludwig Wittgenstein have Asperger's syndrome? *European Child & Adolescent Psychiatry, 9*(1), 61–65. https://doi.org/10.1007/s007870050117

Gauthier, D. (1974). Justice and natural endowment: Toward a critique of Rawls's ideological framework. *Social Theory and Practice, 3*(1), 3–26. https://doi.org/10.5840/soctheorpract1974318

Kymlicka, W. (2001). *Contemporary political philosophy: An introduction* (2nd ed.) Oxford: Oxford University Press.

Lareau, A. (2011). *Unequal childhoods: Class, race, and family life* (2nd ed.) Berkeley, CA: University of California Press.

Merry, M. (2008). Educational justice and the gifted. *Theory and Research in Education, 6*(1), 47–70. https://doi.org/10.1177/1477878507086730

Nagel, T. (1997). Justice and nature. *Oxford Journal of Legal Studies, 17*(2), 303–321. doi:10.1093/ojls/17.2.303

Nozick, R. (1974). *Anarchy, state, and Utopia*. Basic Books.

Pogge, T. (1989). *Realizing Rawls*. Ithaca, NY: Cornell University Press.

Rawls, J. (1971). *A theory of justice*. Cambridge, MA: The Belknap Press.

Rawls, J. (1999). *A theory of justice: Revised edition*. Cambridge, MA: The Belknap Press.

Rawls, J. (2001). *Justice as fairness: A restatement*. Cambridge, MA: The Belknap Press.

Sardoc, M. (2019). Talents and distributive justice: An interview with Hillel Steiner. *Educational Philosophy and Theory, 51*(14), 1393–1398.

Sandel, M. (2007). *The case against perfection: Ethics in the age of genetic engineering*. Cambridge, MA: The Belknap Press.

Satz, D. (2007). Equality, adequacy, and education for citizenship. *Ethics, 117*(4), 623–648. https://doi.org/10.1086/518805

Shiffrin, S. (2010). Incentives, motives, and talents. *Philosophy & Public Affairs, 38*(2), 111–142. https://doi.org/10.1111/j.1088-4963.2010.01180.x

Smith, S. R. (2005). Keeping our distance in compassion-based social relations. *Journal of Moral Philosophy, 2*(1), 69–87. https://doi.org/10.1177/1740468105052584

Steiner, H. (2002). Silver spoons and golden genes: Talent differentials and distributive justice. In D. Archard & C. Macleod (Eds.), *The moral and political status of children* (pp. 183–194). New York, NY: Oxford University Press.

Swift, A. (2003). *How not to be a hypocrite: School choice for the morally perplexed parent*. London: Routledge.

Against selection: Educational justice and the ascription of talent

Johannes Giesinger

ABSTRACT
This essay starts from the observation that the issue of talent, in relation to the problem of distributive justice, can be approached from two different angles. First, it is common to discuss the justificatory function of talent, that is, its role in the justification of educational or social inequalities. In addition, however, this essay proposes to look at practices of talent ascription and their causal role in the distribution of educational prospects. These practices tend to exacerbate educational inequalities due to social background, especially when they are tied to selective educational settings. There is reason to avoid talent-based selection in education, in order to contain the negative effects of practices of talent ascription.

The notion of talent figures in widely discussed accounts of distributive justice, such as John Rawls's principle of fair equality of opportunity,[1] or Harry Brighouse and Adam Swift's meritocratic conception of educational justice that is inspired by Rawls's principle:

> An individual's prospects for educational achievement may be a function of that individual's talent and effort, but it should not be influenced by her social class background. (Brighouse & Swift, 2008, p. 447)

This conception mentions three factors influencing educational achievement: talent, effort, and social background. It is assumed that those educational inequalities due to talent and effort are legitimate – but not those due to social background. Within this framework, then, the notion of talent plays a role in the justification of distributive inequalities. I call this its justificatory function.

The issue of talent, in relation to questions of distributive justice, can also be approached from another angle, namely by looking at practices of talent ascription. In educational contexts, we lack direct access to people's talents, but often ascribe talent (or lack of talent) to students. This is done in educational everyday practice as well as when important decisions regarding students' educational or professional future are taken – that is, when they are selected for specific educational programmes, schools, or school types on the basis of an ascription of talent or ability. As I would like to make clear in this essay, practices of talent ascription are morally problematic, in part with regard to their distributive effects. The upshot is that regardless of how we understand the notion of talent and its justificatory function in a theory of distributive justice, the moral problems of practices of talent ascription are so serious that we have reason not to rely on them to ground the distribution of educational prospects. The ascription of talent cannot and should not be avoided, in educational contexts. What can be avoided, however, is setting up selective structures within which educational benefits are allocated on the basis of talent ascriptions.

In the first section, I outline how the justificatory function of talent is seen, in recent liberal debates on distributive educational justice.[2] The second section addresses the issue of talent ascription, while the third section spells out the argument against selection.

Talent – its justificatory function

As already mentioned, talent has a justificatory function in the meritocratic conception of educational justice, where it is named as one of the legitimate sources of educational inequality. In Brighouse and Swift's – as well as Rawls's – view, this means that people with equal talents should have equal educational prospects. It is thus unjust when equally talented students do not have access to the same educational institutions, or are not provided with the same amount of educational resources, due to differences in social backgrounds. In this reading, the meritocratic approach does not amount to the idea that the talented have a moral claim to be educationally or socially privileged over the less talented. It does not require us to spend more resources on the talented than on other groups, or to establish special educational programmes for their benefit.

Apart from that, neither Rawls nor Brighouse and Swift see the meritocratic principle as the only principle in their conception of (educational) justice. Starting with Rawls, liberal theorists have questioned the justificatory role of talent in theories of distributive justice. The main line of critique is that talent itself is 'undeserved', in the sense that talented people have done nothing to bring it about, and therefore cannot take credit for it. They are not more responsible for their talent than they are for their family background. Both (natural) endowment or talent and the conditions of upbringing are – to use Rawls's expression – 'arbitrary from a moral point of view' (Rawls, 1971, p. 65), and cannot justify educational or social inequalities.

There are several ways to take up this critique of the justificatory role of talent in the development of principles of educational justice. The first approach has been labelled 'luck egalitarianism', as it makes the justification of inequality dependent on whether it is due to brute luck, or to responsible decisions and actions (e.g., Arneson, 1989; Cohen, 1989). As talent is a question of luck, it cannot justify educational inequalities. Effort, by contrast, seems to be rooted in people's responsible decisions. One possible formulation of the luck egalitarian conception of educational justice is, then, that

> [a]n individual's prospects for educational achievement should be a function of that individual's effort, but it should not be influenced by her social class background or her level of talent. (Brighouse & Swift, 2014a, p. 17)

This 'radical' conception – as Brighouse and Swift call it – requires a neutralization of all educational inequalities due to natural talent: students with different talent should all have the same educational prospects. It must be further clarified what is meant by an equality of educational prospects. One possible reading is that all students who show equal effort should reach the same level of achievement, regardless of their talents. This view raises both moral and practical problems, as it seems to demand that talented students should be held back in the development of their potential. This might be seen as morally problematic if it means we deny students an education that fits their specific needs (Merry, 2008). It is also questionable in practical terms: denying students appropriate conditions of learning in the school context might not hinder them from promoting their abilities outside of this context, for example by reading books by themselves. So, it is not clear that it is even possible to hold students back from developing their potential.

There are other ways to specify the luck egalitarian approach in education. It all depends on *what* it is that is to be equalized – it might not be achievement, but resources, opportunities, or educational quality (Calvert, 2014). Focusing on one of these alternatives makes the account less 'radical' than the version just outlined. For instance, the demand to provide students with equal educational resources, irrespective of talent and social background, leaves room for talented students to reach a higher level of ability and to benefit from their talent, especially with regard to competition for social positions.

Even the 'radical' interpretation of the luck egalitarian account, however, might be considered as not radical enough. When we go one step further, we arrive at what Brighouse and Swift (2014a) call the 'extreme' egalitarian view, or what Tammy Ben-Shahar (2016) – who defends this position – characterizes as 'all-the-way-equality'. According to this conception, only strict equality of educational outcome can count as legitimate. There is an obvious argument for this move, given the Rawlsian view on 'moral arbitrariness': it can be argued that especially in children, effort is not primarily a question of personal decisions, but is more likely due to natural preconditions and family background. Clearly, a student's motivation and ambition are highly influenced by attitudes towards education that are transmitted within the family. We can come to the conclusion that not only are those inequalities due to talent and social background unjustified, but also those rooted in effort. There is no room, then, for legitimate inequalities of educational achievement.

Ben-Shahar's argument for strict equality focuses on the 'positional' value of education. In the competition for attractive social positions, the value of education for one person is positional in the sense that it depends on how well others are educated. Being better qualified than others matters, in this regard, irrespective of one's actual level of achievement. The worse qualified are worse off simply due to their relative position in the distribution of education. Against this backdrop, Ben-Shahar claims that only strict equality of achievement can be considered fair, as any inequality can put the worse off in a disadvantaged position. She explains, in addition, that 'prioritarian' views developed on the basis of Rawls's difference principle must come to the same conclusion, as regards the distribution of positional benefits (see also Brighouse & Swift, 2006). According to the difference principle, social and economic inequalities are legitimate to the extent that they benefit the worst off. As Ben-Shahar writes,

> when positional goods are concerned, equality will always benefit the worst-off and is therefore justified from a prioritarian point of view. Inequality in education could never be justified by a principle of priority [...], simply because there is no possible case in which unequal educational outcome would be better for the worst-off than equality. (2016, p. 87)

In Rawls's view, positional inequalities due to talent and effort are legitimate. Rawls develops the difference principle to complement the principle of fair equality of opportunity, as a remedy for its shortcomings. As indicated, Rawls acknowledges the moral arbitrariness of the natural distribution of talent. However, he refuses to react to it by endorsing a luck egalitarian or even more extreme principle. Instead, he claims that the difference principle should be applied on the basis of the (meritocratic) principle of fair equality of opportunity. This amounts to the view that the naturally talented should be allowed or encouraged to develop their potential, but should at the same time be required to use it for the benefit of all, especially the worst off in society. Talent should not be considered as people's individual property, but as a 'common asset' (Rawls, 1971, p. 101). So, while the meritocratic principle demands that equally talented people should be treated equally, in education, the difference principle might be used to determine how groups of equally talented people should be treated compared to each other. As Rawls puts it,

> the difference principle would allocate resources in education, say, so as to improve the long-term expectation of the least favored. If this end is attained by giving more to the better endowed, it is permissible; otherwise not. (Rawls, 1971, p. 101)

The difference principle, then, gives us reason to provide special attention to the 'least favored' – those with little talent. We might try to improve their (educational) situation by spending additional resources on them. Gina Schouten (2012) has proposed, in her prioritarian approach to educational justice, that with regard to children with serious natural learning disabilities, we should not focus on making them (positionally) competitive, but should enable them to develop capacities that contribute to their flourishing, more broadly understood. However, directly promoting the education of the worst off might not always be the best way to benefit them, if we follow Rawls; they might be benefitted by providing special educational attention and resources to the 'better endowed', who are thereby enabled to develop their potential to the advantage of everyone in society. After all, the less talented depend on the talented developing their potential and taking on important responsibilities in society, for instance as political or economic leaders or as scientific or artistic innovators. Some inequalities in education might be justified, then, if they ultimately work out to the advantage of the worst off in society. Brighouse and Swift go one step further, when they say that '[w]e should also be willing to sacrifice meritocratic principles where it is necessary to benefit the less advantaged, all things considered' (Brighouse & Swift, 2008, p. 463). They propose giving up the meritocratic demand to treat equally talented people equally, if this is to the advantage of the worst off in society.

We have seen, so far, two different ways to deal with the weaknesses of the meritocratic principle – it can be transformed into a more demanding egalitarian principle, or complemented by a prioritarian account. In the debate on educational justice, the critique of the meritocratic idea has also led to a type of approach that turns away from the demand for distributive equality, favouring instead a notion of relational (democratic, civic) equality, combined with the demand for a 'sufficient' or 'adequate' education (Anderson, 2007; Satz, 2007). The basic idea is that all people should be enabled to reach a threshold level in the development of relevant capacities that enables them to live as equals, in the liberal democracy, and is in this regard adequate. Within this framework, the notion of talent lacks a justificatory function, as the standard of adequacy applies to everybody, regardless of natural or social preconditions. The adequacy view accounts, in some sense, for the view that both types of disadvantage are undeserved. However, it does not require social and natural disadvantages to be fully neutralized. It demands equality with reference to a given threshold, not strict equality of outcome. Inequalities above the threshold are seen as legitimate, irrespective of how they come about: they might be the result of unequal financial resources, or differences in natural endowment. In this view, then, promoting the talented and thereby creating significant educational inequalities might be legitimate.

To sum up, then, the liberal debate on educational justice provides us with some room for privileging talented people over others. However, it is widely understood that talent in itself does not form the basis of a moral claim for social reward. Also, there is a general view that inequalities due to social background are to be reduced. Given that there are in fact vast social inequalities in education, there is likely to be wide agreement among adherents of different distributive principles that improving the situation of the socially disadvantaged should be one of the main aims of education policy.

Talent ascription as a moral problem

Let us now turn to the second issue mentioned in the introduction – the moral problem of talent ascription. It is natural that talent is ascribed to students, by teachers, other students, or their parents. To ascribe talent means to make assumptions regarding students' potential. It is to assume what they can or will learn, under the right social and educational circumstances. These ascriptions might refer to how fast and easily students learn new things, but also to the level of achievement they can be expected to reach, given their willingness to make an effort. Sometimes the concept of talent is used to depict the highly gifted, while other usages are more broad, referring to all kinds of students and their potential. Typical usages rely on a distinction between talent and effort, as related to actual levels of achievement. We might speak about someone as being talented, but lacking the effort to develop her talents, and thereby explain this person's poor level of achievement. We might also say that someone who performs poorly while making a huge effort lacks talent. While statements of this kind are common, especially in selective school settings, they can be highly problematic.

A first point is that it is not clear that talent is, as is often assumed, an innate and fixed property of human beings. Clearly, people's natural endowment influences their capacity for learning. But should we say that it is naturally determined from the outset what capacities a person can acquire, and what level in the development of these capacities she can reach? It has been claimed that a person's talent is partly due to social factors (see Meyer, 2014). Israel Scheffler (1985, p. 11) speaks of the 'myth of fixed potentials', assuming that in the course of a life, new potentials can arise, while others can vanish. He assumes that a person's potential is neither naturally nor socially determined, but evolves through their individual agency in a symbolically structured world (see also Benner, 1987).

To question the innate and fixed character of talent does not mean that talent ascriptions, as ascriptions of learning potential, are to be considered as altogether inappropriate. It only means that by ascribing talent we do not refer to fixed properties, but to individual traits that have partly been brought about by social and educational experiences, and are likely to further evolve. Talent ascriptions, then, cannot be considered to be definite judgements about people's potential, but only as short-term predictions that are tied to a specific educational context: Teachers will typically have some competence in predicting whether a student can be successful within the educational environment they know and help shape.

The question of what talent 'is' and how it evolves must be distinguished from the epistemic question of how it can be identified in students. Even if we assume that there are fixed talents, it is not clear how they can be tracked. The problem is that what we experience (or measure) are students' actual performances, not their talents. We take their performances as an index for their capacities and/or their talents. It should be pointed out, furthermore, that measuring performance is itself unreliable, as success or failure in a test is strongly shaped by the type of test itself, and the conditions of testing. In testing students, we find out how they perform in a particular test situation.

There is, then, a general epistemic issue here that can be considered one of the sources of a specific form of injustice in selective educational practices. It is widely documented that children from socially privileged backgrounds are more likely to be accepted in schools or programmes for talented students. This is the case, for instance, in the selective school systems of the German-speaking countries, where socially disadvantaged students are strongly under-represented in the most demanding school type (the Gymnasium) (see, for example, Baumert & Schümer, 2001; Baumert, Stanat, & Waterman, 2006). It can also be observed in programmes of gifted education (Card & Giuliano, 2016; Grissom & Redding, 2016; Peters & Engerrand, 2016). One explanation for this phenomenon is that children from privileged families perform better in school, presumably because they are more able or 'talented'. This is what is sometimes characterized, following Raymond Boudon (1974), as one of the primary effects of social background. It is explained with reference to differing social or educational experiences of children within the family. To cite an example often used by Harry Brighouse and Adam Swift (2014b), well-educated parents tend to advantage their children by reading bedtime stories to them.

In selection processes, however, there are also so-called secondary effects of social background (Boudon, 1974): students from different backgrounds who show similar levels of achievement are treated differently. This might be explained in a variety of ways, for instance by pointing to the fact that students or their parents make different educational choices depending on their social background. I would like to focus on another factor (that might be indirectly linked to parents' or students' choices), namely, the ascription of talent by teachers and other professionals within the education system.[3] There is reason to believe that practices of talent ascription are permeated by prejudice, stereotypes, or bias – to use the different terms that have become common in ethical debates on race and gender. Recently, feminist theorists have drawn on psychological research to shed light on specific kinds of bias that woman and other social groups face (esp. Fricker, 2007; Anderson, 2012; Saul, 2013). In the educational context, girls have long been seen as a disadvantaged group, and there is still debate on girls' performance in areas such as mathematics that are stereotyped as 'male'. However, nowadays, it is not girls but socially disadvantaged and immigrant children that seem most disadvantaged in the education system. Also, there is concern regarding the educational achievement of boys who are often considered as less ambitious than girls.

Stereotypes are best understood as 'widely held associations between a group and an attribute' (Fricker, 2007, p. 31). This means that they entail 'some empirical generalization about a given social group' (ibid.). In our case, the attribute in question is academic ability or talent, or the lack thereof. Some groups – such as the socially disadvantaged – are seen as less talented than others. Stereotypes can play out as explicit ascriptions, but in educational contexts, they are more likely to occur as an implicit form of bias. This means that teachers may explicitly deny having such stereotypes, but nevertheless be influenced by them in the ascription of talent (Anderson, 2012, pp. 167–168; Brownstein & Saul, 2016).

One interesting empirical finding is that people (for example teachers) who are committed to the idea of fixed talents are more susceptible to be biased in their talent ascriptions. These people tend to think that talent is something that you have or lack, and they relate this notion to the idea that some groups are by nature more talented than others. By contrast, those who do not think of talent as a natural limit to individual development seem less prone to stereotypical talent ascriptions (Levy et al., 1998; Steele, 2010, pp. 168–169). In this way, then, the (implicit) theory of what talent 'is' can become effective in practices of talent ascription, regardless of which theory is adequate.

Talent ascriptions influenced by stereotypes are *epistemically* wrong, in that they fail to appropriately represent the true potential of students. It is more difficult to say whether or in what sense they are *morally* wrong. It would be clear if teachers were intentionally disadvantaging some groups of students, and had explicitly degrading attitudes towards them. Mostly however this is not the case. Many teachers only want the best for all their students, whatever their social background, ethnicity, colour, or sex. Many of them try to overcome their implicit bias. It is dubious, then, whether they can be morally blamed for their epistemically wrong judgements.

Nevertheless, it might be seen as appropriate to say that some students are morally wronged by biased talent ascriptions. For one, it could be suggested that these ascriptions are in themselves morally wrong, irrespective of possible consequences. One way to elucidate this view is to say that students are wronged when their true potential is not recognized. They are, then, not taken for what they are, and what they are able to do. This seems especially troubling when the reason is their belonging to a disadvantaged group. We might also say that students are wronged when they are not treated in accordance with the merit-based rules of educational practice: if a selective decision is set up as based on achievement, you are treated unfairly if you are excluded from an attractive programme or school due to factors that have nothing to do with your talent or performance.

Biased talent ascriptions might also be morally wrong because of the negative effects they can have on a person's individual development or career. In a general way, it can be empirically expected that negative talent ascriptions have a negative effect on the students' learning processes, whether they are epistemically accurate or not. If these effects exist, it is questionable what empirical accuracy means in this regard, as the ascription itself possibly changes what the student can or will learn.

A related issue is that widely held stereotypes – whether teachers explicitly communicate them or not – can have an effect on learning, to the extent that they are internalized by learners. This is what is characterized as *stereotype threat* in social psychology (Steele, 2010). For instance, when girls take up the view that girls are bad at maths, this will eventually influence their performance in this field. To describe this phenomenon, we might also use Sally Haslanger's notion of discursive construction (Haslanger, 2012): the ascription of certain traits causally brings them about, as the ascriptions are endorsed by the people themselves. This creates a 'feedback loop', as these individuals start acting correspondingly, and the said traits are further ascribed to them.

Against this background, we can view the distributive effects of practices of talent ascription. The basic claim is that practices of talent ascription themselves tend to exacerbate social inequalities in education. There are two ways in which this can happen. First, practices of talent ascription might refer to traits that are socially brought about, and second, the judgements themselves might be distorted by bias.

It might well be that the ascription of talent to people adequately captures some traits that they in fact possess. The problem is that these traits – whether we speak of 'capacities' or 'talents' – might themselves have developed through social and educational processes. By ascribing talent to some students, then, we might react to social privileges that these students have had so far in their lives. This might positively impact their development, as their self-esteem and motivation is improved. To the extent that talent ascriptions are relevant for selective decisions, being labelled as 'talented' can go along with further advantages: in programmes or schools specially set up for the talented, these students can be appropriately challenged, and provided with learning opportunities that fit their educational needs.

In addition, the ascription of talent might be epistemically inadequate in the sense that it misrepresents the traits or potentials of students as a result of implicit bias. Here, students' social disadvantage does not stem from their actual traits, but from their belonging to a social group which is subject to negative stereotypical ascriptions of talent. Group membership, then, triggers a biased reaction on the part of teachers. As outlined, biased talent ascriptions can have further consequences, and eventually impact students' future performance and the development of their capacities. This is especially the case when students adopt stereotypical ascriptions of talent (or lack of talent) to their own social group, and are influenced by them in their performance.

To sum up, talent ascriptions might be morally problematic in a variety of ways. First, they might be seen as wronging people, regardless of their effects on them. Second, they might be considered as harming people in their learning processes. Third, they can be seen as having problematic distributive effects.

Against selection

In my further considerations, I draw on my rough conclusion from the first section, and bring it together with my remarks about practices of talent ascription in the second section.

Educational inequalities due to social background, prevalent across our societies, are considered morally problematic by adherents of different liberal conceptions of educational justice. There is widespread agreement that the impact of social background on educational achievement ought to be reduced. As has become clear, practices of talent ascription tend to play a causal role in bringing about certain distributive effects that are commonly seen as problematic. These practices tend to exacerbate educational inequalities due to social class and family background in two different ways. First, they react to traits and performances that are already influenced by social background, and second, they may themselves be biased.

Even if we uphold the idea of talent as innate and fixed, then, we might think of practices of talent ascription as distorting educational justice. Consider again the meritocratic principle in which the notion of natural talent obtains a justificatory function regarding the distribution of educational prospects. As defenders of this principle, we might assume that treating students differently due to differences of talent is legitimate, but nevertheless acknowledge that practices of talent ascription are among the social factors that tend to undermine meritocratic justice.

How should we react to this moral problem? A natural idea is to address the issue on the individual level. If it is true that teachers are often epistemically incorrect in their ascription of talent, partly due to their biased view of students, they should improve their ability to make talent assessments first and foremost. In the first place, this means that teachers should rid themselves of their biases towards certain social groups. It might be demanded, in this regard, that teacher training should focus on this point, enabling (future) educators to make appropriate judgements of their students' abilities or talents.

As practices of talent ascription are a constitutive aspect of teaching, improving individual diagnostic competence is crucial. The question is whether it is enough. Consider, in this context, the debate on epistemic justice, and in particular Miranda Fricker's account of what she calls 'testimonial injustice' (Fricker, 2007). A person is victim of testimonial injustice, in Fricker's view, when she is not considered to be credible in what she says due an 'identity prejudice' towards her as a member of a disadvantaged group. Clearly, testimonial injustice – being about credibility and knowledge – differs from the injustice at work in talent ascription.[4] But the two are also related, as both involve the assessment of people's competence or ability. Supposedly, the very same groups who are victims of testimonial injustice are also systematically underestimated in their talent.

In Fricker's view, it is mainly up to the individual to overcome her prejudice: people should reflect on their prejudiced judgements, and try to correct them. They should develop specifically epistemic virtues. However, as prejudice often works unconsciously, as implicit bias, it is especially difficult to detect and correct (Anderson, 2012; Alcoff, 2010). Elizabeth Anderson states that we cannot fully rely on the epistemic improvement of individuals, but must also address the problem on the structural level. Anderson identifies social inequality, combined with the segregation of social groups, as the main structural source of epistemic injustice. She recommends policies to foster social integration, including the provision of better educational opportunities for marginalized groups (Anderson, 2007; 2012, pp. 169–171). These are structural measures thought to fight prejudice in society.

The proposal that I would like to make is not set up to *extinguish* biased talent assessment, but to reduce its role. As indicated, talent ascription becomes especially consequential with regard to the distribution of educational prospects when it is tied to selective educational structures, that is, institutional settings that stipulate a distribution of educational opportunity on the basis of talent or 'merit'. By abolishing – or not establishing – selective settings in education, the negative impact of talent ascription with regard to educational justice might thus be contained.

Where selective schools or programmes exist, teachers cannot escape an assessment of students' talent and their fitness for a particular programme. In this way, their alleged bias tends to influence students' (and their parents') decision-making, especially when it confirms widespread social views of particular social groups, and students' or parents' own view of themselves. By releasing teachers from the duty of selecting students on the basis of talent ascription, we allow them to shift their focus – from the identification of the talented to the question of how talent in all students is best promoted.

At this point, defenders of selective schooling might bring up another structural proposal, namely, that access to selective programmes should be regulated on the basis of anonymous tests that exclude the impact of bias. As the experience shows, for example in German-speaking areas where such tests regulate access to the Gymnasium, this kind of system does not significantly reduce the impact of social background on educational success. One reason is, of course, that the level of achievement (or 'talent') at the time when the test is taken is already influenced by the social conditions of the student's upbringing. Another reason is that members of disadvantaged groups who might in fact be able to pass the test may refuse to take it. This is in part due to teachers failing to encourage them to take it, or they themselves underestimating their own abilities or talents. As the work on stereotype threat shows, individuals might also underperform in the test itself due to a biased view of their own ability.

Conclusion

In the liberal debate on distributive justice, it is widely agreed that being talented does not go along with a direct claim for educational or social advantages. It is also commonly understood that educational inequalities due to social background ought to be reduced. As has become clear in this essay, practices of talent ascription tend to exacerbate such inequalities, especially in connection with selective educational settings. It can therefore be seen as a moral imperative to minimize the impact of talent ascriptions on the distribution of educational prospects by refraining from the establishment of selective programmes or schools.

Notes

1. Rawls (1971, p. 73) introduces this principle as follows: '[W]e might say that those with similar abilities and skills should have similar life chances. More specifically, assuming that there is a distribution of natural assets, those who are at the same level of talent and ability, and have the same willingness to use them should have the same prospects of success regardless of their initial place in the social system.' Note that while Rawls uses the concept of talent here, he also speaks of people's 'abilities', 'skills', and 'natural assets'. He also makes clear here that he regards effort ('the willingness to use' one's talents) as a legitimate source of inequality.
2. I will not consider libertarian or conservative positions on this issue, but restrict myself to the liberal debates that have their origin in John Rawls's work on distributive justice (Rawls, 1971).
3. Bos et al. (2004) have shown, in an empirical study, that teachers' recommendations at the end of the fourth school year - which serve as the basis for the allocation of students to the different school types in the German system - are significantly influenced by factors that have nothing to do with ability or performance.
4. Krassimir Stojanov (2016) has a different view: he claims that students are victims of testimonial justice in Fricker's sense when their potential is underestimated. The educational significance of Fricker's account is also discussed by Ben Kotzee (2013, Kotzee, 2017).

Disclosure statement

No potential conflict of interest was reported by the author(s).

References

Alcoff, L. (2010). Epistemic identities. *Episteme*, *7*(2), 128–137.

Anderson, E. (2007). Fair opportunity in education: A democratic equality perspective. *Ethics*, *117*(4), 595–622. doi:10.1086/518806

Anderson, E. (2012). Epistemic justice as a virtue of social institutions. *Social Epistemology*, *26*(2), 163–173. doi:10.1080/02691728.2011.652211

Arneson, R. (1989). Equality and equality of opportunity for welfare. *Philosophical Studies*, *56*(1), 77–93. doi:10.1007/BF00646210

Baumert, J., & Schümer, G. (Eds.) (2001). Familiäre Lebensverhältnisse, Bildungsbeteiligung und Kompetenzerwerb. In: *PISA 2000. Basiskompetenzen von Schülern und Schülerinnen im internationalen Vergleich* (pp. 323–407). Leske und Budrich.

Baumert, J., Stanat, P., & Watermann, R. (Eds.) (2006). *Herkunftsbedingte Disparitäten im Bildungssystem: Vertiefende Analysen im Rahmen von PISA 2000*. VS Verlag für Sozialwissenschaften.

Benner, D. (1987). *Allgemeine Pädagogik: Eine systematisch-problemgeschichtliche Einführung in die Grundstruktur pädagogischen Denkens und Handelns*. Juventa.

Ben-Shahar, T. H. (2016). Equality in education: Why we must go all the way. *Ethical Theory and Moral Practice, 19*(1), 83–100.

Bos, W., et al. (Eds.) (2004). Schullaufbahnempfehlungen von Lehrkräften für Kinder am Ende der vierten Jahrgangsstufe. In *IGLU: Einige Länder der Bundesrepublik Deutschland im nationalen und internationalen Vergleich* (pp. 191–228). Waxmann.

Boudon, R. (1974). *Education, opportunity, and social inequality: Changing prospects in western society*. Wiley.

Brighouse, H., & Swift, A. (2006). Equality, priority, and positional goods. *Ethics, 116*(3), 471–497. doi:10.1086/500524

Brighouse, H., & Swift, A. (2008). Putting educational equality in its place. *Education Finance and Policy, 3*(4), 444–466. doi:10.1162/edfp.2008.3.4.444

Brighouse, H., & Swift, A. (2014a). The place of educational equality in educational justice. In K. Meyer (Ed.), *Education, justice, and the human good* (pp. 14–33). Routledge.

Brighouse, H., & Swift, A. (2014b). *Family values. The ethics of parent-child relationships*. Princeton University Press.

Brownstein, B., & Saul, J. (Eds.). (2016). *Implicit bias and philosophy* (Vol. 2). Oxford University Press.

Card, D., & Giuliano, L. (2016). Can universal screening increase the representation of low income and minority students in gifted education? *Working Paper 21519*. National Bureau of Economic Research.

Cohen, G. A. (1989). On the currency of egalitarian justice. *Ethics, 99*(4), 906–944. doi:10.1086/293126

Fricker, M. (2007). *Epistemic injustice. Power and the ethics of knowing*. Oxford University Press.

Grissom, J., & Redding, C. (2016). Discretion and disproportionality: Explaining the underrepresentation of high-achieving students of color in gifted programs. *AERA Open, 2*(1), 233285841562217–233285841562225.

Haslanger, S. (2012). *Resisting reality: social construction and social critique*. Oxford University Press.

Kotzee, B. (2013). Educational justice, epistemic justice, and leveling down. *Educational Theory, 63*(4), 331–349. doi:10.1111/edth.12027

Kotzee, B. (2017). Education and epistemic justice. In I. J. Kidd. (Ed.), *The Routledge Handbook of Epistemic Injustice* (pp. 324–335). Routledge.

Levy, S., Dweck, C. S., & Stroessner, S. J. (1998). Stereotype formation and endorsement: The role of implicit theories. *Journal of Personality and Social Psychology, 74*(6), 1421–1436. doi:10.1037/0022-3514.74.6.1421

Merry, M. S. (2008). Educational justice and the gifted. *Theory and Research in Education, 6*(1), 47–70. doi:10.1177/1477878507086730

Meyer, K. (2014). Educational justice and talent advancement. In K. Meyer (Ed.), *Education, Justice and the Human Good* (pp. 133–150). Routledge.

Peters, S. J., & Engerrand, K. G. (2016). Equity and excellence: Proactive efforts in the identification of underrepresented students for gifted and talented services. *Gifted Child Quarterly, 60*(3), 159–113.

Rawls, J. (1971). *A theory of justice*. The Belknap Press.

Satz, D. (2007). Equality, adequacy, and education for citizenship. *Ethics, 117*(4), 623–648. doi:10.1086/518805

Saul, J. (2013). Implicit bias, stereotype threat and women in philosophy. In: F. Jenkins & K. Hutchison (Eds.), *Women in Philosophy: What needs to change?* (pp. 39–60). Oxford University Press.

Scheffler, I. (1985). *Of human potential. An essay in the philosophy of education*. Routledge & Kegan Paul.

Schouten, G. (2012). Fair educational opportunity and the distribution of natural ability: toward a prioritarian principle of educational justice. *Journal of Philosophy of Education, 46*(3), 472–491. doi:10.1111/j.1467-9752.2012.00863.x

Steele, C. (2010). *Whistling vivaldi and other clues to how stereotype threat affects us*. New York/London.

Stojanov, K. (2016). Educational justice as respect egalitarianism. *Critique and Humanism Journal, 46*(2), 249–260

Talents, abilities and educational justice

Kirsten Meyer

ABSTRACT

The assumption that students are differently talented often underlies the public and philosophical debate about the justice of school systems. It is striking that despite the centrality of the notion of 'talent' in these debates, the concept is hardly ever explicated. I will suggest two explications: First, philosophers who point to different talents often assume that these are somehow fixed potentials that pose limits to what someone can achieve. According to this understanding, no matter how hard someone tries, she simply cannot perform well due to a lack of talent. Second, talking about different talents can be understood as saying that two students who will receive the same amount of educational resources are nevertheless expected to perform differently in the future. In the public as well as the philosophical debate it is common to assume that educational prospects should be equalized when it comes to unequal social backgrounds, but not when it comes to unequal talents. In this paper, I put into question three reasons that could speak in favor of this assumption: the first refers to the connection between talents and limits, the second to the relation between talents and the transformation of resources and the last one to the idea that talents somehow go back to the person's true self.

1. Different talents and equal educational opportunities

The assumption that students have different talents influences the setup of school systems. Some schools offer special courses for students who are assumed to be more talented than others. In several countries, there is also a division between different types of schools which builds on the assumption that students are divided by talent. Furthermore, this assumption influences the philosophical debate on educational justice as well as more general debates in political philosophy. These debates deal with the question of whether or not, or to what extent, talent may influence the prospects of educational achievement or chances for well-being.

Within political philosophy, authors often distinguish natural talent from social class background as two distinct factors relevant for social justice. For example, John Rawls' principle of fair equality of opportunity in *A Theory of Justice* is limited to 'those who are at the same level of talent and ability' and who have 'the same willingness to use them' (Rawls, 1999, p. 63). Rawls uses a combination of the principle of fair equality of opportunity and his so-called 'difference principle' to keep the advantages that come with higher levels of talent and ability within bounds (pp. 63–64). He also points out that talents are morally arbitrary (p. 65). Moreover,

Rawls does not merely deal with educational opportunities and prospects of educational achievements, but rather with offices and positions open to all. Since Rawls does not really have an education-focused notion of equality of opportunity, its implications for education are not entirely clear. Despite these difficulties in interpreting Rawls, however, his original conception of fair equality of opportunity is at least similar to the following meritocratic principle of equal *educational* opportunities: 'An individual's prospects of educational achievement may be a function of that individual's effort and talents, but they should not be influenced by her social class background'.[1]

Unequal educational opportunities, thus understood, could theoretically be compatible with benefitting the less advantaged in society. When wealthy parents are permitted to buy better educational opportunities for their children (e.g. by paying for them to attend elite private schools) this could enhance the total stock of human capital in society. These productivity gains could be redistributed in order to benefit the less advantaged. However, against this line of argument Brighouse and Swift point out that aside from the doubtfulness of the alleged productivity gains and their potential advantages for everyone, education influences an individual's prospects of gaining attractive jobs, status, and control over work. All of this also has a strong impact on a person's subjective well-being (Brighouse & Swift, 2014, p. 22). For these reasons, Brighouse and Swift believe that equal educational opportunities do indeed ultimately work to the benefit of the less advantaged in society. Rawls (1999) also seems to hold that a lack of equal educational opportunities is altogether worse for the less advantaged: 'They would be justified in their complaint not only because they were excluded from certain external rewards of office but because they were debarred from experiencing the realization of self which comes from a skillful and devoted exercise of social duties. They would be deprived of one of the main forms of human good'. (p. 73).

If this is the case however, why should the demand for equal educational opportunities be restricted to equal educational opportunities *for the equally talented*?[2] Why is it just her social class background that should not influence a person's educational opportunities? Why is it less problematic if her prospects of educational achievement are a function of her talents? One reason could be that it is not possible to even out the prospects for educational achievement for differently talented individuals. Since this cannot be done, it makes no sense to demand that it is done for reasons of justice. In the next paragraph, I will critically discuss this assumption and reveal that a clearer focus on the notion of talent is needed in order to evaluate it.

2. What are talents?

In the current philosophical discussion, some authors talk about 'developed talents' or 'adopted talents' as well as of 'natural talents' and 'inborn talents' (e.g. Anderson, 2004, pp. 101–102; Brighouse & Swift, 2014, p. 17; Giesinger, 2011, p. 43; Satz, 2007, p. 630). In general, however, most authors in debates on educational justice just refer to 'natural' talents when they use this term (e.g. Calvert, 2014; Sachs, 2012; Shields, 2015). Moreover, most authors have a static rather than dynamic concept of talent where talents are assumed to be somehow fixed.

The concept of talent is closely related to performance and achievement. Talents are what enable or facilitate future achievements. A reference to the talents of a person does not point to current skills or other traits that a person may have, but rather to the future acquisition of these traits. For example, high mathematical talent can enable someone to develop high mathematical abilities in the future. Future achievements, such as musical or mathematical abilities, do not just go back to a person's genes. They also go back to the fruitful instructions of a highly qualified math teacher or to parents that are dedicated to math themselves. Therefore, some authors criticize the reference to 'natural' talents for neglecting these external circumstances. For example, Vopat (2011) points out that talent should be attributed to the environment in which the child was raised: 'In families that seem to produce more talented individuals, researchers have shown that the environment in which the child was raised accounts for his or her ability, and not the genetic pool from which they came' (p. 63). Even if the genetic endowments may play *some* role, they are surely not decisive for future achievements.

Educational achievements, such as mathematical abilities, do not just go back to the natural endowments of a person. These educational achievements enable or facilitate further achievements, such as the development of even higher abilities. Mathematical abilities that enable the development of even higher mathematical abilities are also identified as 'talents' to develop these higher abilities. As soon as any of these abilities are visible, they are the result of the upbringing of a person. This speaks in favor of a concept of developed talents rather than natural talents and of dynamic rather than static talents.

A person has a talent to reach a certain educational goal (e.g. the development of a certain ability) if this person can reach this goal in a sufficiently good educational environment. Thus, talents are potentials to reach educational goals. For example, when a child enters school, she may have the potential to become very good at mathematics. This potential is itself acquired and the result of an educational process. In taking over this perspective, one need not deny that the natural endowments somehow contribute to this potential. One can acknowledge the biological dimension and still emphasize that it was not sufficient to acquire the actual potential, and that all kinds of environmental factors must have been in place to do so. A current potential to acquire certain abilities later on depends on the current abilities and the predicted circumstances up to that point in time. For the prediction of what a person can achieve in the future, a mere reference to her natural endowments is not instructive. This prediction rather goes back to her actual abilities and the expected future circumstances.

Thus to denote certain talents is to say something about a tendency toward future achievements. Developed talents are potentials for future achievements that are based on actual abilities that are themselves developed. Moreover, these potentials can change over time. For instance, a person who has experienced the feeling of being good at something can benefit from that by acquiring additional potentials in other areas. Scheffler (1985) formulates this as follows: 'A girl who is potentially good at mathematics becomes a different person with actual achievement of mathematical skill. New potentials arise with the realization of the old; ways of thinking about related topics are now open to her that were formerly closed. New feelings of confidence may contribute to potentials for other sorts of learning as well' (p. 11).

To ascribe a potential cannot be understood as predicting categorically that it will be realized (Scheffler, 1985, p. 46). Instead, Scheffler thinks that we refer to the potential of a person in order to emphasize that it is possible for her to develop certain abilities or that it is easier for her than for others to develop these abilities. I will have a closer look at these two points in the following two sections.

2.1. Talents and the limits of what a person can achieve

If a person is said to have the 'talent' to develop certain abilities it is possible for her to develop these abilities, because there are no obvious constraints. This means that it is neither literally impossible nor extremely unlikely for her to develop them. Thus if a person has the potential to develop an ability, it must be realistically possible for her to develop this ability in a certain amount of time with a certain amount of resources. She must have the appropriate internal and external resources to develop the ability.

If a person does *not* have the potential to develop an ability, she cannot develop this ability even if she would like to develop it. To say that that a person has no *natural* talent often means that her natural endowments set *limits* to what she can do. Humans cannot naturally fly or acquire the ability, thus having no natural talent for flying (Brighouse, 2014, p. 16). Usually, a reference to the lack of talent is more specific, though. The point is not that humans *as humans* lack certain talents (such as a talent for flying), but that specific individuals lack certain talents.

For example, Anderson (2007) points out that 'every student with the potential and interest should receive a K–12 education sufficient to enable him or her to succeed at a college that prepares its students for postgraduate education' (p. 597). We can read 'every student *with the potential*' as saying that there are students who would not succeed at a college even if they tried and had the appropriate external resources. They simply cannot succeed since they do not have the potential for it.

The reasons for these obstacles are often assumed to go back to a lack of *natural* talent. However, these obstacles can also be acquired. Someone may lose a potential due to external circumstances, such as a lack of education. This is also something Scheffler (1985) emphasizes: 'Certain educational moments must be caught or they are gone forever' (p. 12). Potentials can disappear because of a lack of external resources or because one did not make use of them.

I may have had the potential to become a good piano player when I was born. However, since I have not played the piano for the last forty years, I no longer have the potential to become a proficient piano player today. Whether or not I did have the potential earlier in my life is a counterfactual question about different courses my life could have taken (what if I had practiced the piano every day for several hours?). Whether or not I did have the *natural* talent is the least meaningful question here. When I was born someone could have said that I have the potential to become a good piano player. The reasons for this prediction, however, would have been the circumstances of my upbringing and not my biological constitution. Only if the natural constraints on my potential to play the piano where unusually obvious (e.g. if I was born without arms and hands), a reference to natural constraints and to a lack of *natural* talent would have been plausible. Despite such unusual cases, a prediction of certain obstacles by a mere reference to our natural endowments is hardly ever possible.

If someone has the potential to develop certain abilities, there are no obvious constraints on developing them at a given point in time (e.g. no obvious constrains today to acquire higher mathematical skills in the future). This point in time is the moment when one attributes the talent; what we thereby take into consideration are the current abilities, such as current mathematical skills. The potential to acquire further abilities, however, can change over time. Someone may lose a potential, but someone may also acquire a potential that is not visible at a given point in time. One may not be able to predict that someone will be able to acquire certain skills, but this may nevertheless happen due to unforeseeable future circumstances. At a later point in time, this may become more obvious and thus one may change one's prediction about what someone can possibly achieve.

Thus, it is not the case that a lack of talent just goes back to natural constraints. The limits to what a person can achieve are not just the results of her natural endowments; the developed talent is also the result of a person's social circumstances. I do not deny that its development is based on genetic preconditions that may differ from individual to individual. Inequalities of natural endowments might be obstacles to educational achievements. However, in most cases, the obstacles at a given point in time will not just go back to natural endowments. They also go back to the social circumstances of the respective individuals up to that point and depend upon the social circumstances from that point onwards.

2.2. Different talents, same resources, different results

In the last paragraph, I started with the notion of (natural as well as developed) talents as *limits*. They enable future achievements, whereas the lack thereof sets the limits of what a person can possibly achieve in the future. A focus on talents as limits, however, cannot account for the comparative notion of talent that we refer to when we speak of someone being more or less talented than others. Brighouse (2014) points to this aspect when he talks about inequalities in people's talents: 'All it means to say that two people are unequally talented is that they have innate characteristics that interact with the environment to produce differences in capabilities' (p. 16).

The idea is that differences in talents entail differences in later achievements. We can apply this idea to natural as well as to developed talents. Let us consider two persons A and B. Their developed abilities A_1 and B_1 at t_1 interact with the environment in distinct ways and thus lead to different abilities at t_2. If a person is more talented than the other, she can reach more on a scale of skills (e.g. on a scale of mathematical skills; from low to high) or she can achieve more with less resources. The first possibility points to certain limits again. Some children cannot reach the high end of the scale, no matter how much they try and how good their future education will be. The latter points to different ways of transforming educational resources into abilities. With the same future exercise and training, some children will achieve a higher level of skills than others. Having more talent, thus, means that given the same educational input (e.g. the same amount of time for practice or the same instructions by a teacher) a higher level of skill is likely to be achieved. Talking about talent here refers to the way in which a person can use educational resources.[3]

Given the same educational resources, a more talented child will learn more in a given amount of time than a comparatively less talented child. Even if a child does not have better mathematical skills than another at the time of entering school, she can have a higher ability to follow the math teacher's instructions. The child's potential at t_1, thus, contains a further present ability at t_1: the ability to use and transform the teacher's instructions for the development of future abilities. This present ability to use the given educational resources is also not just a product of the child's natural talents but greatly depends on her upbringing and developed characteristics, e.g. a sense of self-worth.

Thus, a common way of speaking about talents and potentials refers to the idea that the same amount of educational resources or practice can lead to different educational results. For example, by referring to unequal mathematical talents, we explain why two children who were given the same amount of teaching have developed different levels of mathematical skills. This does not say anything, though, about the limits of what a child can possibly achieve given maximum input. If one of the children were given extra time for practice or additional teaching, she might have reached the same level of mathematical ability as the other one.

To sum up this point, I distinguished between the concept of talent as a limit to what a person can possibly achieve and the concept of talent as a facilitator of future achievements. According to the latter, if two children are equally talented at t_1, they will foreseeably perform equally well at t_2 if they receive the same educational resources and invest the same amount of time into their learning process until t_2. However, if the lesser talented child receives educational resources of a higher quality until t_2, she may perform equally well at t_2. In this case, both of the children might have acquired the same ability to process future input by the math teacher (for instance, because the formerly slower learner has now gained enough confidence to be able to pick up the teacher's explanations as quickly as the other one). As a result, even though they had different degrees of talent at t_1, they are equally talented at t_2. The formerly less talented child now has acquired new abilities and thus both children now have the same capacities for future achievements. Therefore, at t_2 they have the same developed talent.

There are two ways to respond to the unequal talents of persons A and B. First, one can aim at equal educational achievements of A and B at t_2 despite their differences in talents at t_1. Second, one can allow the unequal educational achievements at t_2 that follow from their different talents. The assumption that unequal talents justify unequal educational success is widely shared. But why are natural or developed talents allowed to influence the educational success? Why do so many people assume that educational prospects should be equalized when it comes to unequal social backgrounds, but not when it comes to unequal talents? In the following sections I will discuss three reasons that could speak in favor of this assumption: the first refers to the connection between talents and limits (3), the second to the relation between talents and the transformation of resources (4) and the last one to the idea that talents somehow go back to the person's inner capacities and true self (5). I will show though, that these reasons are largely to be rejected.

3. Missing talents as limits to more equality?

Why should one aim at equal educational prospects when it comes to unequal social backgrounds, but not when it comes to unequal talents? One reason seems to be that educational prospects cannot be equalized, because due to a lack of talent there are limits of what some pupils can possibly achieve.

The focus on the allegedly *natural* limits of what a person can achieve often leads to the assumption that these limits are inalterable. This explains why talents are often seen as fixed limits, but it offers no justification for this view. A child that has fewer capacities than other children when entering school will in many cases be able to achieve the same educational results – she might just need more time and resources. The limits of what this child can achieve also depend significantly on external circumstances. Thus altering these circumstances (e.g. to give more resources to children who lack certain capacities when entering school) can change these limits.

The philosophical discussion often explicitly or implicitly presumes that humans are born with unequal talents. This static notion of talent entails that talents cannot be changed. In rejecting this position, one might take the opposite stance and claim that unequal educational success is *entirely* due to unequal external conditions. According to this view, a person's environment is decisive for her development of individual capacities. Varying external conditions thus explain the differences in educational outcomes. Talents are not just a natural contingency but changeable and not predetermined. This notion of talent contrasts the static view by presenting the human individual as a mere product of cultural practices and social interaction, rather than one of primarily genetic disposition.

In contrast to these extreme positions, it is plausible to assume that both genetic predispositions and external conditions play a relevant role in shaping a child's physical and mental development. A restricted focus on natural endowments is usually inappropriate in order to explain the genesis of the actual abilities. These developed abilities go back to the natural endowments as well as to the external circumstances. In light of their close interaction since early embryonic development however, it is almost impossible to consider these factors separately. These aspects cannot be separated from each other. For this reason, Howe (2015) even calls a mere reference to natural talents 'illusive': '[N]atural talents are illusive. They have no manifestation independent of environmental influences; they function as unobserved posits used to explain differences in observed human performance' (p. 188). One cannot acquire new natural talents and one cannot acquire a developed talent for which one did not have the necessary natural talent. However, the influence of the natural endowments on this developed talent is in most cases invisible and often overstated.

It is often impossible to decide which limits stem from genetic disposition and which go back to socialization. Especially when trying to detect the supposedly 'natural' differences between people, we are faced with this epistemic difficulty. But even if this problem were to be solved, it remains to be shown why the distinction should be relevant at all. In many cases it seems to be irrelevant by what means the limits are brought about. Why should it matter whether a child is not able to graduate in the following eight years due to a lack of *natural* talents or because she was not properly *cared for* in the first years of her life? For this particular child, obviously, this is not important anymore.

Of course, this is different when we are considering children who have just recently been born or are yet to be born. We could try to make sure that the opportunities they have at this early point in life persist, e.g. by arranging the school system accordingly. Equality of opportunity can then be understood as demanding that only the unchangeable sets limit to what a person can achieve. On this basis we could demand to spend more resources on early age support and education, to support families in poverty and to make sure that a child's opportunities for social participation are not undermined right at the beginning. Limits to what individuals can achieve are not only due to natural dispositions but largely depend on external conditions. It is important to be aware of the possibility to change these factors.

Moreover, even natural endowments do not necessarily set absolute limits. A lack of natural talent might just make the attainment of specific educational goals costlier or more time-consuming. A reference to a lack of talent is often meant to denote the limits of what a person can achieve in the future. Combined with a focus on *natural* talents, this suggests that these limits are given by fixed natural constraints that cannot be overcome. This conception of fixed potentials is often misleading. Not only do a person's natural endowments set the limits of what she can achieve in the future, but these limits are also set by the external circumstances from now on. Moreover, her current developed talent could have been different if the external circumstances would have been different up until now. This diagnosis may not matter for her future educational success (her potential may nevertheless be irretrievably lost), but it matters for the question of how we organize the educational process for *other* future children (such that they do not lose their potential due to the impoverished external circumstances). Furthermore, even for *this* person, the potential for future achievements may *not* be lost, if she receives an extra amount of educational resources in the future. A reference to a lack of *natural* talent can be misguiding since it neglects this possibility.

In many cases it is just a matter of the expense at which an individual can accomplish a specific educational goal. A less talented student might need more time and effort to achieve the same outcome than another one. But it is not just the student who will have to put in extra effort. Additional educational resources will be needed, e.g. more detailed instructions by a teacher. With the same amount of educational resources, a more talented student can achieve more. Are we supposed to compensate for this fact by providing the less talented with more educational resources? Or should everyone receive the same amount of educational resources? I will have a closer look at these competing positions in the next section.

4. Meritocratic conceptions and educational resources

The meritocratic conception holds that one should aim at equal educational prospects when it comes to unequal social backgrounds, but not when it comes to unequal talents. In the following, I will argue that a focus on *developed* rather than *natural* talents and a focus on talents as *facilitators* rather than *limits* challenge this view.

We have seen that the term 'talents' often denotes the limits of what an individual (who supposedly lacks that talent) can possibly achieve, even with a large amount of resources. Moreover, I pointed out that talents influence the amount of resources that an individual needs for acquiring a certain degree of performance and achievement. Differently talented individuals are not equally effective in translating resources into abilities. Thus two equally talented children who enter school might foreseeably perform equally well at a later stage if they receive the same amount of educational resources from now on. Two differently talented children might foreseeably perform differently at a later stage if they receive the same amount of educational resources.

The meritocratic conception does not speak in favor of equal educational outcomes for differently talented children. It allows natural talents to be influential even if the differences in natural talents would not constitute a limit to what is possible. If the differences in natural talents where relevant to the amount of resources one had to invest in order to achieve certain educational outcomes, then the meritocratic conception did not tell us to invest more resources into the education of the lesser talented children. According to the meritocratic conception, educational results are allowed to depend upon talent and effort, whereas they should not depend on the social class background. Therefore the meritocratic conception allows that those who are differently talented *by nature* receive the same amount of educational resources. The meritocratic conception just questions the influence of the social background on different educational outcomes (for example, when wealthier parents can buy a better education for their children).

By focusing on developed talents, however, giving more resources to the lesser talented students can also be justified with regard to the meritocratic conception of educational justice. The meritocratic conception holds that one's social class background should not influence an individual's prospects of educational achievement. An appropriate conception of talent reveals the high impact that the social environment has on developed talents. This justifies the demand that educational resources should be distributed assigning a larger share to the less talented. In this respect, proponents of the meritocratic conception should be more sensible to the notion of developed talents.

Moreover, the distinction between talents as *limits* and as *facilitators* could diminish the intuitive credibility of the meritocratic conception. The meritocratic conception might be plausible if one considers natural talents as limits, but with regard to talents as facilitators, it is an open question as to why one should endorse it. If a person with lesser natural talent required more resources in order to reach the same educational result, why should she, from a perspective of justice, nevertheless receive the same amount of educational resources? With the same amount of resources, those who are more talented obtain the better results. From various perspectives of justice, however, the *lesser* talented child should receive *more* educational resources (for an overview about these perspectives and their implications for different talents, see Meyer, 2014, 2016).

With the same amount of resources, the lesser talented child will achieve less. One might justify this by referring to the lack of talent as a limit. If, however, there is no such principled constraint, there are various reasons to give more resources to the less talented, even if they were less talented *by nature*. More importantly, though, the awareness of the impact that the social environment can have on *developed* talents justify the demand that a larger share of educational resources should be given to those who have more difficulties in learning. For example, they should receive a larger share of the teacher's time or they should receive additional resources for smaller classes and highly qualified teachers.

The opposite position demands that those who are *more* talented should be provided with *more* resources to develop these talents. Vopat (2011) judges this idea to be widespread: 'We tend to think that differences in natural talents and abilities justify differences in access to resources. So, when a child exhibits a natural talent that other children lack, providing the resources necessary to develop that ability in the talented child is justified' (p. 65). An important reason for this view seems to be that the development of one's natural talents contribute to the development of one's 'true self'. In the next section, I will elucidate this view more closely and subsequently reject it.

5. Talents and self-realization

The static notion of natural talents refers to a predefined disposition that will unfold under suitable conditions. According to the static notion, this disposition decisively influences school success. From this point of view, the genetic material almost completely predetermines the developmental possibilities of a human being. This static conception assumes that it cannot be influenced by targeted educational and training measures. While these assumptions are not justifiable scientifically (and modern philosophers would not deny this), there is still a dominant focus on *natural* talents within philosophy, and there is a widespread metaphor that fixed talents *unfold*.

Children with high potentials, talents or natural endowments are sometimes said to be 'gifted' (Merry 2008). A person is gifted by her static genome, which is given to her from the beginning of life and which is not the product of a development process. The actual realization of the genetically determined possibilities is said to be promoted by helping the gifted to 'unfold' their talents. Since the talents we identify are *developed* talents though, this metaphor is often not suitable. Our developed talents are not given to us at the time of our birth, waiting to unfold. Instead, our developed talents are the contingent results of the circumstances of our upbringing, and they can change over time.

Furthermore, talents also do not constitute a kind of underlying 'real self', even though this view is widespread. From this perspective, the allegedly gifted individuals should be supported in unfolding their 'self'. Shields (2015) dubs the development of one's talents to a certain extent 'sufficient self-realization' (p. 54). Ben-Shahar (2016) also remarks that '[o]ne could argue that one's talent, ability, and potential are a part of their self, and therefore should not be compromised for the sake of equality' (p. 96).

I do not deny that we should support and enable individuals to develop their talents. The reference to that person's 'self', however, is easily misguiding in this context. Scheffler also has some concerns that are relevant here. He emphasizes that people have different potentials for entirely different things. It is not obvious which of these should be regarded as valuable and thus be declared as 'gifts', 'talents' or her 'true self'. Moreover, a person has different potentials which cannot be jointly realized: 'The potential for the one career and the potential for the other may both be genuinely *possessed* by a given youth but that does not imply that he has the potential for both together. Thus, they are not, alas, jointly *realizable*' (Scheffler, 1985, p. 15).

Thus, it is not at all clear what one should identify as *the* underlying potential of a person that is worth being realized, because it constitutes her 'true self'. Moreover, the self is constituted by autonomous decisions, for instance, when a person decides to *realize* certain potentials. Suppose a child has the potential to become an outstanding musician and suppose we could somehow identify this potential. Would we, in any way, be promoting her 'true self' if we enabled her to accomplish musical excellence? If someone autonomously decides to *not* develop a capability (e.g. by preferring other things over practicing the piano for many hours a day) then this does not seem to be a failure of or a deviation from her true self. And if a lesser talented child has a strong desire to improve her musical abilities, it is not clear why this child should have a weaker claim on musical education than the other child.

It is far from obvious that our potential to develop certain abilities is particularly relevant for our self. Ben-Shahar (2016) explains this as follows: 'Potential can be frustrated for many reasons and therefore it is further away from the core of people's identities than the abilities which they actually possess' (p. 96). Furthermore, there is no reason to assume that only our *natural* talent makes us who we really are. If this where the case, then the most significant moment for one's true self would be at the time of birth. At this point in time, the environment has had the least impact on one's potentials. But we would not assume that for that reason a newborn child is somehow 'closer' to her true self.

I do not want to deny that school education should take into account the children's individual strengths and what they enjoy doing (which also often correlates). Aiming at equal educational outcomes despite different talents seem to disregard individual strengths and interests. But it does not follow that the allegedly natural talent should fully determine educational success, instead pupils should have the possibility to participate in shaping their own path in life. It is important to stress the value of autonomy in education and particularly to let pupils develop the abilities that they identify with the most. Often these will be abilities that a pupil has confidence in, and that she assumes to be able to develop to a relatively high level. It will be those abilities which she finds easy to develop, e.g. when she is able to pick up instructions very easily and learn quickly. In this respect, the self-assessment of one's own talents can be relevant to where one sees oneself in the future. By declaring a pupil to be untalented or less talented however, a school can also obstruct many opportunities for a child. Thus the setup of the school system and individual teachers should not continuously limit children's potentials by denying their 'talents'. Instead, a school should contribute to opening up possibilities and expanding limits in a way to enable children to succeed in what they want to achieve.

6. Conclusion

Talents are potentials to develop certain abilities. A lack of talent entails that a person cannot develop specific abilities; on the other hand, being particularly talented means being able to easily develop a certain ability. Talents are *facilitators* for future achievements, and sometimes a lack of talent also sets *limits* to the possibility of future achievements.

Whether a person can develop an ability and to what level she is able to do so often depends on external factors. Therefore, one should be careful not to be misled by a reference to 'natural talents' and to be too quick in proclaiming limits independent of external circumstances. Equal educational outcomes cannot be pursued by people with unequal natural talents, if some of these talents pose *limits*. They can, however, be pursued by people that are unequal in their natural talents as *facilita*tors. In addition, one should acknowledge that the talents we identify are *developed* talents. They are not fixed, can change over time and with additional resources, differences in developed talents can diminish.

A person's talents should also not be associated with her 'nature' or 'true self' that unfolds when her talents are developed. Schooling should take into account individual strengths and interests, no matter if these are due to 'natural' talents or to the circumstances of the children's upbringing. Aside from recognizing individual strengths however, school education should open up possibilities and expand pupils' limits as far as possible, instead of justifying alleged limits by attributing a lack of talent.

Notes

1. Brighouse and Swift (2014, p. 15) call this the 'meritocratic conception' and define it in the same way as I do here. They also state that the meritocratic conception 'is closely related to Rawls's principle of fair equality of opportunity' (Brighouse & Swift, 2014, p. 16). Schouten (2012, p. 473) also claims that we can think of it 'as an education-specific analogue to John Rawls' fair equality of opportunity principle'. For a discussion of different notions of equal opportunity, including equal *educational* opportunity, see Meyer (2016).
2. This restriction is very common. A rare exemption is Ben-Shahar (2016), who explicitly argues for equal educational outcomes.
3. This is also how Kollar and Loi (2015) explain the concept of talent: 'A has more talent than B means that she needs less exercise and training of an ability in order to achieve equally good results, other things being equal' (p. 38).

Acknowledgement

We acknowledge support by the Open Access Publication Fund of Humboldt-Universität zu Berlin.

Disclosure statement

No potential conflict of interest was reported by the author(s).

References

Anderson, E. (2004). Rethinking equality of opportunity: Comment on Adam Swift's How not to be a hypocrite. *Theory and Research in Education*, *2*(2), 99–110. https://doi.org/10.1177/1477878504043438

Anderson, E. (2007). Fair opportunity in education: A democratic equality perspective. *Ethics, 117*(4), 595–622. https://doi.org/10.1086/518806

Ben-Shahar, T. H. (2016). Equality in educational outcome: Why we must go all the way. *Ethical Theory and Moral Practice, 19*, 83–100.

Brighouse, H. (2014). Response: Education, justice, ideal theory, and non-ideal theory. In M. S. Moses (Ed.), *Philosophy of education* (pp. 15–20). Colorado, IL: Philosophy of Education Society.

Brighouse, H., & Swift, A. (2014). The place of educational equality in educational justice. In K. Meyer (Ed.), *Education, justice, and the human good: Fairness and equality in the education system* (pp. 14–33). Abingdon: Routledge.

Calvert, J. (2014). Educational equality: Luck egalitarian, pluralist and complex. *Journal of Philosophy of Education, 48*(1), 69–85. https://doi.org/10.1111/1467-9752.12048

Giesinger, J. (2011). Education, fair competition, and concern for the worst off. *Educational Theory, 61*(1), 41–54. https://doi.org/10.1111/j.1741-5446.2011.00390.x

Howe, K. (2015). The meritocratic conception of educational equality: Ideal theory run amuck. *Educational Theory, 65*(2), 183–201. https://doi.org/10.1111/edth.12106

Kollar, E., & Loi, M. (2015). Prenatal equality of opportunity. *Journal of Applied Philosophy, 32*(1), 35–49. https://doi.org/10.1111/japp.12067

Merry, M. (2008). Educational justice and the gifted. *Theory and Research in Education, 6*(1), 47–70. https://doi.org/10.1177/1477878507086730

Meyer, K. (2014). Educational justice and talent advancement. In K. Meyer (Ed.), *Education, justice and the human good: Fairness and equality in the education system* (pp. 133–150). Abingdon: Routledge.

Meyer, K. (2016). Why should we demand equality of educational opportunity? *Theory and Research in Education, 14*(3), 333–347. https://doi.org/10.1177/1477878516676709

Rawls, J. (1999). *A theory of justice: Revised edition*. Cambridge, MA: Harvard University Press.

Sachs, B. (2012). The limits of fair equality of opportunity. *Philosophical Studies, 160*(2), 323–343. https://doi.org/10.1007/s11098-011-9721-6

Satz, D. (2007). Equality, adequacy, and education for citizenship. *Ethics, 117*(4), 623–648. https://doi.org/10.1086/518805

Scheffler, I. (1985). *Of human potential: An essay in the philosophy of education*. London: Routledge & Kegan Paul.

Schouten, G. (2012). Fair educational opportunity and the distribution of natural ability: Toward a prioritarian principle of educational justice. *Journal of Philosophy of Education, 46*(3), 472–491. https://doi.org/10.1111/j.1467-9752.2012.00863.x

Shields, L. (2015). From Rawlsian autonomy to sufficient opportunity in education. *Politics, Philosophy and Economics, 14*(1), 53–66. https://doi.org/10.1177/1470594X13505413

Vopat, M. C. (2011). Magnet schools, innate talent and social justice. *Theory and Research in Education, 9*(1), 59–72. https://doi.org/10.1177/1477878510394811

Earning rent with your talent: Modern-day inequality rests on the power to define, transfer and institutionalize talent

Jonathan J. B. Mijs

ABSTRACT

In this article, I develop the point that whereas talent is the basis for desert, talent itself is not meritocratically deserved. It is produced by three processes, none of which are meritocratic: (1) talent is unequally distributed by the rigged lottery of birth, (2) talent is defined in ways that favor some traits over others, and (3) the market for talent is manipulated to maximally extract advantages by those who have more of it. To see how, we require a sociological perspective on economic rent. I argue that talent is a major means through which people seek rent in modern-day capitalism. Talent today is what inherited land was to feudal societies; an unchallenged source of symbolic and economic rewards. Whereas God sanctified the aristocracy's wealth, contemporary privilege is legitimated by meritocracy. Drawing on the work of Gary Becker, Pierre Bourdieu, and Jerome Karabel, I show how rent-seeking in modern societies has come to rely principally on rent-definition and creation. Inequality is produced by the ways in which talent is defined, institutionalized, and sustained by the moral deservingness we attribute to the accomplishments of talents. Consequently, today's inequalities are as striking as ever, yet harder to challenge than ever before.

Introduction

Capital makes the world go 'round. Those who own it reap the rewards. Many of the largest companies in the world are in car manufacturing (Toyota, Volkswagen), petroleum refining (Exxon Mobil, Royal Dutch Shell), and other industries that rely on copious amounts of capital. Social science research describes how ownership of capital is a major source of wealth inequality (Keister & Moller, 2000; Killewald et al., 2017; Piketty, 2014). Scholarship points to the unfair advantages capital ownership provides, such as the ability to extract rent beyond its productive value (Atkinson, 2015; Sørensen, 2000, 1996; Weeden & Grusky, 2014). Moreover, capital is passed down intergenerationally to sons and daughters whose only accomplishment is being born to the right set of parents. Some of the wealthiest people in the world today owe their fortune to their family business. From the Waltons (Wal-mart) and Bettencourts (L'Oreal), to the Mars family and the Koch brothers, today's rich belong to the same social groups, networks, and families as those who held the reins generations ago (Chetty et al., 2014; Pfeffer & Killewald, 2018).

While scholars, journalists and politicians are scrutinizing the ownership, transmission, and use of capital, much of modern-day inequality has a different guise. Whereas we disapprove of the plutocracy of capital, we celebrate the meritocracy of talent (Littler, 2018; Mijs, 2019; Mulligan, 2018b). The last decades have seen the rise of companies based on little more than great ideas, and a top one percent of athletes, pop stars, managers and executive officers, whose fortunes derive from their unique set of skills and abilities. Today, six out of the ten largest equities in the Standard & Poor 500 are IT companies built on the creativity, entrepreneurship, and hard work of extraordinary individuals. We speak of talent when an athlete outperforms the competition, when a young politician rises through the ranks of their party, or when two guys in a garage[1] set up what turns out to be one of the largest companies in the world. We laud talent, we love those who have it, and we loathe our own limits; if only we had come up with that idea first, we'd be the Bill, Larry, Sheryl or Oprah with a billion dollars to our name.

There is a shadow side to the meritocracy of talent. In the world of talent, success is driven by good ideas, ambition, and hard work. Inequality simply reflects their uneven distribution: some of us are brighter, aim higher, work harder. It is a compelling story, but one with cruel consequences. When talent is the basis for success, and differences in talent are the source of economic fortune, what right do we have to complain about inequality and its excesses? Looking at society through the lens of talent equates success with merit, failure with incompetence. Talent consecrates people's privileged place in society (Accominotti, 2018; Khan, 2010). Talent today is what inherited land was to feudal societies; an unchallenged source of symbolic and economic rewards. Whereas God sanctified the aristocracy's wealth, contemporary privilege is legitimated by talent. Consequently, today's inequalities are as striking as ever, yet harder to challenge than ever before.

In this article, I argue that talent and capital have much more in common than meets the eye. I will show that the economic gains of talent rely on a process of rent-seeking previously reserved for the owners of capital. In what follows, I give a brief history of rent to show how the return on talent relies on three processes, none of which are meritocratic: (1) just like capital, talents are intergenerationally transmitted from parents to children; (2) further, what constitutes talent relies on the definitional power of powerful gatekeepers who decide which traits to reward and which to discard; (3) moreover, talents are structural, not individual traits; their economic returns are institutionalized in privileged positions. In sum, I will show that inequality is produced by the ways in which talent is defined, transmitted, and sustained by the moral deservingness we attribute to the accomplishments of talents.

A short history of rent

The word rent, to most people, is a reminder of their monthly commitment to a landlord or landlady; the price that comes with the roof over their head. For others, it is a source of income: property owners extract rent by letting real estate to people or businesses willing to pay more than their upkeep requires. We tend to associate the term real estate with houses, and the agents selling them, but it actually refers to buildings as well as land. Whereas it is ownership of the former that is especially important in today's urban societies, for most of human history land has been the primary source of income and wealth.

Economic theory describes how, starting with David Ricardo's law of rent. Ricardo (1817) defines rent as the individual benefits accrued by owning land, over and above its productive quality. Land, if used for agricultural purposes, for instance, has a productive quality. Ownership of the land however has its own benefit: the ability to extract additional returns in the form of rent. Such benefits derive from artificial limits to the supply of an asset, like in a monopoly (see Marshall, 1895). Given a fixed supply of land, the owners can extract returns that greatly exceed its value in a competitive market.

Whereas Ricardo's law of rent continues to inform economic thought, the industrial revolution and the coming of post-industrial society (Bell, 1973) meant the concept of rent required an update. Jacob Mincer (1958), Theodore Schultz (1960), and, most notably, Gary Becker (1962) provide the foundation for that by taking the concept of capital to the labor market and to the realm of education. Human capital theory states that our minds and bodies are potential sources of rent as well. To Becker, human capital is how most modern citizens make a living; the market rewards people's investments in productive skills, knowledge, habits and traits:

> 'Schooling, a computer training course, expenditures of medical care, and lectures on the virtues of punctuality and honesty [are] capital. That is because they raise earnings, improve health, or add to a person's good habits over much of his lifetime. Therefore, economists regard expenditures on education, training, medical care, and so on as investments in human capital. They are called human capital because people cannot be separated from their knowledge, skills, health, or values in the way they can be separated from their financial and physical assets.' (Becker, 2002)

Whereas the focus of human capital theory is on the productive quality of education and health, minds and bodies can also be a source of rent. For one, the supply of human capital is artificially limited. As Becker and others have acknowledged, people are not equally positioned to reap the rewards of investments in human capital. Potential investments in human capital are limited by financial constraints, which are a function of the cost of schooling (and the cost of health, among other productive qualities) and opportunities to invest; i.e. the availability of and access to pre-schools, private tutoring and extra-curricular activities, elite colleges, etc. Simply put, you can't accumulate human capital if you cannot afford school or get in.

The human capital equation however is missing a crucial variable, to which I now turn. Rent-seeking in the age of human capital rests on talent.

Returns = investment * talent

No amount of schooling will turn a half-wit into a genius. Equally, Einstein may have written his theory of relativity even if he hadn't graduated from high school (which, some sources suggest, he barely did).[2] In other words, some talent is required for schooling to make an impact. In fact, there are good reasons to suspect that a higher level of available talent is likely to produce greater returns on the invested education.

To start, schools are set up to cater specifically to students' talents, either by adjusting the level and pace of learning to students' abilities or by differentiating instruction altogether by sorting students into general and honor's classes, vocational and academic tracks, and other forms of grouping based on ability (Domina et al., 2017; Mijs, 2011; Van de Werfhorst & Mijs, 2010). Moreover, a student's talents determine whether particular educational opportunities are or aren't available. For instance, remedial classes are offered only to students with learning difficulties, while a great deal of talent is required for a person to be given the opportunity of receiving an Ivy League education as elite institutions purposefully keep enrollment low (more on this point below).

In short, *real* returns on education equal investment *times* talent. Minds and bodies become a source of rent when ideas and skills are deemed unique talents which merit a reward beyond their productive qualities. In what follows, I show that there is nothing necessary or natural about talent's economic returns. Just like other forms of capital, talents (1) are intergenerationally transferred; (2) rely on being so defined by powerful gatekeepers; and (3) are institutionalized in positions of privilege and protected professions.

We receive our talents from our parents

Reflective of the classical Greek meaning of the word τάλαντον (money), we receive our talents from our parents. Academic ability, IQ, health, height, and physical attractiveness are just a few of the many traits unequally distributed by the rigged lottery of birth (Fischer et al., 1996;

Rimfeld et al., 2018). On top of the genetic gains of birth are a set of social skills—or 'cultural capital' to use Bourdieu's (1984) term. Children acquire from their parents and from their *social milieu* more generally, traits and manners, a sense of entitlement or constraint, and a level of (dis)comfort with adults and authorities, which makes school a much more productive space for some than for others. Upper (middle) class parents tend to instill in their children the cultural capital to set them up well for tests and exams (Bourdieu, 1984; Yamamoto & Brinton, 2010), dream big and aim high (Jackson, 2013; Lareau, 2011), and assure that teachers give them the attention they demand (Calarco, 2011, 2018).

In Bourdieu's words, by failing to take into account the investments already made within the family,

> [Human capital theorists] let slip the best hidden and socially most determinant educational investment, namely, the domestic transmission of cultural capital. Their studies of the relationship between academic ability and academic investment show that they are unaware that ability or talent is itself the product of an investment of time and cultural capital. (Bourdieu, 1986, pp. 244–245)

In other words, talent is inherited, in the strict sense, to the extent that our intellectual ability, health, and other productive traits are based on the genetic makeup we receive from our parents. In a broader sense as well, children's talents depend on their parents (Smeeding et al., 2011). Children rarely make investment decisions themselves; the amount of time, attention and resources parents commit to education ('shadow education') greatly impacts their children's human capital accumulation (Buchmann et al., 2010). Taken together, there are vast and consequential differences in people's opportunity to benefit from human capital and extract rent, because of the unequal distribution of talent and early investments therein. Talents, in short are far from the individual quality we make them to be; talent, like capital, is transferred, sustained and cultivated across generations.

Talent is whatever is so defined

When Ivy League colleges invented American Football around 1880, a new set of talents was created with it. Some such talents travel better than others; being a good football (soccer) player may earn you respect and, if you're good enough, a living, in as many as 200 countries with professional football leagues. Being good in *American Football*, by contrast, means much more in one country than anywhere else.

The portability of talent points to a crucial quality: talent's meaning and payoff is context-specific, varying across place and over time.[3] What is true for American Football is true for musical craft and artistic talent; and even for the traits that people value in others. As I have argued elsewhere (Mijs, 2016, p. 20), what constitutes merit is historically contingent and institutionally-specific:

> Manliness, aggression, asceticism and (bi)sexuality, for instance, were considered important traits for men to have in Sparta, 400 BC, and display of such traits was rewarded with social status (De Botton, 2005). In Western Europe anno 479, in contrast, pacifism, vegetarianism and asexuality were considered meritocratic traits (ibid.). Similarly changes in meritocratic traits over time are described with regard to the rise of court society (Elias, 1939), in the evaluation of American social science and humanities scholarship (Tsay et al., 2003), as well as between men and women today (Prentice & Carranza, 2002).

What is termed, considered and concomitantly rewarded as productive traits, skills and knowledge depends on how such are defined by society's gatekeepers. So does the opportunity to earn rent with your talent.

A powerful empirical illustration of this insight comes from Karabel's (2005) archival research at Harvard, Princeton and Yale. Digging through their archives, he uncovered detailed minutes and reports describing how in the post-World War I era these elite institutions discussed and devised strategies for keeping out unwanted groups of students, while keeping their gates open to the students they wanted to have. How? By defining merit in ways that their preferred students could meet, but others couldn't. First they included 'character' in the admission criteria as a way to exclude Catholics, then they introduced additional requirements in the form of recommendation letters and personal interviews as a means to weed out the uninitiated. As a means of last resort, they incorporated athleticism into their definition of merit to raise the barrier for purportedly physically-unfit Jewish students.

The take-away from Karabel's study is that definitions of talent are never neutral; how we define qualities like talent, character and merit always benefits some groups of people, while putting others at a disadvantage. Consequently, an important basis of rent-seeking lies with those who are in a position to define talent. The definition of talent does not stop at the front-gate; schools continuously draw boundaries between groups of students (e.g. 'vocational,' 'academic,' 'gifted,' 'at-risk') (Golann, 2015). For those fortunate to fit the mold, these boundaries can produce powerful credentials (degrees) and distinctions (e.g. 'magna cum laude'). In the worst-case-scenario, they lead to a student's expulsion, the long-term consequences of which have been described as a 'school-to-prison pipeline' (Kim et al., 2010; Mittleman, 2018; Welch & Payne, 2018).

This definitional power extends far beyond the realm of education, into the world of literature (Franssen & Kuipers, 2013), fashion (Mears, 2010), business (Khurana, 2002), and as we will see below, sports.

Talents are institutionalized in positions of privilege

Some definitions of talent fluctuate; others are more stable. The main process by which definitions are made to stick is through institutionalization: the rent-producing quality of talent is incorporated in positions that generate rent. Simply put, in order to turn your labor power into money, you need a job or a market for your services. Without either, your hard work and talent will go unrewarded.

Sports offer a good illustration of this process. The ability to jump high, dribble and throw a bouncing ball was institutionalized in the sport of basketball in 1891. Before that time, playing basketball was just that: play. With the institutionalization of the sport, that ability became a skill, and with the establishment of the National Basketball Association in 1946 that skill became a productive quality. As the sport's popularity grew, its valuation rose. Today, a professional basketball player in America can make as much as $45 million in a season, not taking into account the lucrative sponsorship deals that supplement athletes' salaries.

That dollar figure is the result of a very long process of rent-creation. In fact, that process is still ongoing. Every number of years, players and teams come together to negotiate just how much their talents are worth. Players today make a lot more than what they made a few decades ago, and players in the US make a multitude of what players in other countries make. The difference is the level of institutionalization of the sport and the rent-creation that came with it. Rent, in sports, is the difference between an athlete with and one without a job. Whereas the difference in skills, effort and talent may be minimal, the difference in reward is likely to be enormous. Owing to 'superstar' markets (Rosen, 1981), a very small group of athletes (Lewis & Yoon, 2018), college graduates (Clotfelter, 2017), fashion models (Mears, 2011), and rock stars (Krueger, 2005) takes home a disproportional part of the pie. As Mulligan (2018a, p. 178) puts it, superstar earnings 'drive a wedge between contribution and desert.'

In more mundane spheres of life as well, people benefit from institutionalized positions of privilege. Certain professions for instance are protected by what Freidson (1970, 2001) calls 'labor market sheltering': strategies for limiting entry into certain professional groups, such as bar exams for lawyers and board exams for doctors. Such practices allow for professional groups to extract advantages beyond the market-value of their human capital. Through such entry requirements, occupational societies set limits to the number of people allowed into their profession, thereby putting a cap on the supply-side of the equation that sets their wages.

Another way occupational groups establish rent-seeking is by institutionalizing demand for their services through government licensing and other forms of occupational closure (Sørensen, 1996). When you go to court, you would do well to get an attorney. In fact, in most countries, you will be provided with one, if needed, on the government's dime. Less obvious is the need, institutionalized in many countries around the world, for a (notary) lawyer when purchasing a house, accepting an inheritance, merging two businesses, translating a government document, or transferring an Internet domain. All these monopolistic services derive from government regulation successfully fought for by occupational groups and societies (see Abbott, 1988).

Yet another source of rent-seeking is in hiring and pay-setting institutions that do not operate on market principles. CEO wages are set by a board of directors who have an interest in appeasing the person whose salary they control (Bebchuk & Fried, 2009; Weeden & Grusky, 2014). When a board of directors hires a CEO, they may in earnest be picking the most meritorious candidate. They are unlikely however to have a lot to choose from. The pool of candidates is limited by a long list of structural forces that keep people from rising through the corporate ranks (Khurana, 2002). The CEO market, in other words, is a closed market:

> Closure generates an artificial scarcity of candidates who are considered for the CEO job. The function of closure is not only to limit the competitive field in this way but also to set the terms of competition and to assign the rewards for work done in accordance with these limits. It creates the rules of the game, constituting the boundaries by which people will be judged and criticized. At its core, then, the external CEO labor 'market' operates as a circulation of elites within a single, sealed-off system relying on socially legitimated criteria that—contrary to conventional economic wisdom—are not to be confused with relevant skills for the CEO position. (Khurana, 2002, p. 205)

In sum, many of the accomplishments celebrated as individual feats in fact reflect the privileged positions people occupy. Such positions depend on a long process of institutionalization through which occupational groups such as lawyers, doctors and basketball players, have established rent-seeking privileges. In short, it's not people and their talents, but talents and their people.

Conclusion

A growing elite in modern societies has made its wealth not based on their birthright, inherited fortune, or by manifest market manipulations. Today's elite is a meritocracy of great ideas and entrepreneurship, and the special talents of artists, athletes and managerial miracle workers. Or so the story goes.

In this article I have argued that talent in fact relies on structural advantages that have nothing to do with the market nor with merit. The accomplishments of talent rely first on the intergenerational transmission of genetic and cultural endowments from parents to their children. Parents, moreover, provide the cultural competence and economic resources to cultivate their children's productive traits—or lack the means to. In short, both the distribution of and investment in talent depend on the lottery of birth.

The returns on talents further depend on which talents are recognized and rewarded. As illustrated by the history of sports, an American Football player before 1880 was just a guy running around with an egg-shaped ball and a harness on. Today, he can make millions of dollars, given that he's privileged to be playing for an NFL team. Talents, in other words, are institutionally-specific and historically contingent. Much power resides with the persons and institutions that guard the gates of talent.

The opportunity to earn rent from your talent rests on institutional forces. For a person to make an income based on their work, they need a job and a market. Certain types of work have a payoff that far exceeds their market-value. The talents of lawyers, managers, athletes and artists, have been institutionalized in their respective vocations by processes of social closure. Closure artificially limits entry into professions and occupations, increases demand for services, and manipulates their pay to maximize the return on talent. In short, it may be more accurate to speak of talents and their people, than of people and their talents.

Whereas a further exploration of the topic falls beyond the scope of this article, it merits mentioning that the undeserved advantages of inheritance, rent-definition, and rent-creation, discussed in this article, seamlessly coexist with capitalism—best illustrated perhaps by the countless examples of such instances in contemporary America. The neoliberal emphasis on market, competition and responsibility has helped elevate talent to what is arguably society's most celebrated trait (Hall & Lamont, 2013; Littler, 2018). 'Investing' in talent and preventing its 'waste' has become a major policy focus in advanced capitalist societies (Organisation for Economic Co-Operation and Development (OECD), 2008; and see Mijs, 2016, p. 16–17), and deemed the best hope for international development (World Bank, 2010). Paradoxically, then, pro-market ideology has come to support and celebrate an enemy of the market, economic rent, under the thin veil of talent.

In conclusion, when we buy and sell the myth that today's billionaires started with nothing but a garage and a great idea, we miss the moral means for scrutinizing inequality. Looking at wealth and status as the accomplishments of individual talent, removes the ground for public debate and political action. Talent cannot be faulted, nor can it be taxed. Recognizing the socially-constructed nature of talent and its institutionalized power, is the first and necessary step for an interrogation of the economic and symbolic returns on talents in contemporary society.

Notes

1. 'We started our company out of our garage,' serves to convey the notion that all a successful enterprise needs is a good idea and a lot of hard work. It has become such a common phrase that it is now referred to as the garage trope. It features as the origin myth of Amazon, Google, Apple, Microsoft and Hewlett-Packard, among other companies (https://www.inc.com/drew-hendricks/6-25-billion-companies-that-started-in-a-garage.html).
2. Einstein did not master French, which was a required topic in his Swiss high school. This is also the most probable reason he failed to gain admission to the prestigious Federal Technical Institute in Zurich. Biographers however note that Einstein showed early signs of his brilliance in high school, and point also to the role of his home environment where 'manipulations of electricity and magnetism were a daily preoccupation helped set him on a road that led to his first relativity theory' (https://www.nytimes.com/1984/02/14/science/einstein-revealed-as-brilliant-in-youth.html).
3. Another way to express this quality of talent is to think of it, in Bourdieusian terms, as field-specific capital; i.e. the qualities and traits that pay off in a particular (structural) setting (Lamont & Lareau, 1988).

Acknowledgements

I thank Stefan Beljean, Katharina Hecht, Thomas Mulligan, Elisabeth Schimpfössl and one of the two anonymous reviewers for their helpful comments and suggestions, and I begrudgingly accept that the unhelpful comments of the other anonymous reviewer may have actually improved the manuscript.

Disclosure statement

No potential conflict of interest was reported by the authors.

ORCID

Jonathan J. B. Mijs http://orcid.org/0000-0002-7895-0028

References

Abbott, A. (1988). *The system of professions: An essay on the division of expert labor*. University of Chicago Press.

Accominotti, F. (2018). Consecration as a population-level phenomenon. *American Behavioral Scientist*, 1–16. doi:10.1177/0002764218800144

Atkinson, A. B. (2015). *Inequality. What can be done?* Harvard University Press.

Bebchuk, L. A., & Fried, J. M. (2009). *Pay without performance: The unfulfilled promise of executive compensation*. Harvard University Press.

Becker, G. S. (1962). Investment in human capital: A theoretical analysis. *Journal of Political Economy*, *70*(5, Part 2), 9–49. doi:10.1086/258724

Becker, G. S. (2002). Human capital. In D. R. Henderson (Ed.), *The concise encyclopedia of economics*. Liberty Fund.

Bell, D. (1973). *The coming of post-industrial society: A venture in social forecasting*. Basic Books.

Bourdieu, P. (1984). *Distinction: A social critique of the judgement of taste*. Harvard University Press.

Bourdieu, P. (1986). The forms of capital. In J. F. Richardson (Ed.), *Handbook of theory and research for the sociology of education* (pp. 241–258). Greenwood Press.

Buchmann, C., Condron, D. J., & Roscigno, V. J. (2010). Shadow education, American style: Test preparation, the SAT and college enrollment. *Social Forces*, *89*(2), 435–461. doi:10.1353/sof.2010.0105

Calarco, J. M. (2011). 'I need help!' Social class and children's help-seeking in elementary school. *American Sociological Review*, *76*(6), 862–882. doi:10.1177/0003122411427177

Calarco, J. M. (2018). *Negotiating opportunities: How the middle class secures advantages in school*. Oxford University Press.

Chetty, R., Hendren, N., Kline, P., Saez, E., & Turner, N. (2014). Is the United States still a land of opportunity? Recent trends in intergenerational mobility. *American Economic Review*, *104*(5), 141–147. doi:10.1257/aer.104.5.141

Clotfelter, C. T. (2017). *Unequal colleges in the age of disparity*. Harvard University Press.

De Botton, A. (2005). *Status anxiety*. Vintage.

Domina, T., Penner, A., & Penner, E. (2017). Categorical inequality: Schools as sorting machines. *Annual Review of Sociology*, *43*(1), 311–330. doi:10.1146/annurev-soc-060116-053354

Elias, N. (1939). *The civilizing process: The history of manners*. Blackwell Publishing.

Fischer, C. S., Hout, M., Jankowski, M. S., Lucas, S. R., Swidler, A., & Voss, K. (1996). *Inequality by design: Cracking the bell curve myth*. Princeton University Press.

Franssen, T., & Kuipers, G. (2013). Coping with uncertainty, abundance and strife: Decision-making processes of Dutch acquisition editors in the global market for translations. *Poetics*, *41*(1), 48–74. doi:10.1016/j.poetic.2012.11.001

Freidson, E. (1970). *Profession of medicine: A study of the sociology of applied knowledge*. University of Chicago Press.

Freidson, E. (2001). *Professionalism, the third logic: On the practice of knowledge*. University of Chicago Press.

Golann, J. W. (2015). The paradox of success at a no-excuses school. *Sociology of Education*, *88*(2), 103–119. doi:10.1177/0038040714567866

Hall, P., & Lamont, M. (2013). *Social resilience in the neoliberal era*. Cambridge University Press.

Jackson, M. (2013). *Determined to succeed?: Performance versus choice in educational attainment*. Stanford University Press.

Karabel, J. (2005). *The chosen: The hidden history of admission and exclusion at Harvard, Yale, and Princeton*. Houghton Mifflin Harcourt.

Keister, L. A., & Moller, S. (2000). Wealth inequality in the United States. *Annual Review of Sociology*, *26*(1), 63–81. doi:10.1146/annurev.soc.26.1.63

Khan, S. R. (2010). *Privilege: The making of an adolescent elite at St. Paul's School*. Princeton University Press.

Khurana, R. (2002). *Searching for a corporate savior: The irrational quest for charismatic CEOs*. Princeton University Press.

Killewald, A., Pfeffer, F. T., & Schachner, J. N. (2017). Wealth inequality and accumulation. *Annual Review of Sociology*, *43*(1), 379–404. doi:10.1146/annurev-soc-060116-053331

Kim, C. Y., Losen, D. J., & Hewitt, D. T. (2010). *The school-to-prison pipeline: Structuring legal reform*. New York University Press.

Krueger, A. B. (2005). The economics of real superstars: The market for rock concerts in the material world. *Journal of Labor Economics*, *23*(1), 1–30. doi:10.1086/425431

Lamont, M., & Lareau, A. (1988). Cultural capital: Allusions, gaps and glissandos in recent theoretical developments. *Sociological Theory*, *6*(2), 153–168. doi:10.2307/202113

Lareau, A. (2011). *Unequal* childhoods*: Class*, race, and family life, second edition with an update a decade later. University of California Press.

Lewis, M., & Yoon, Y. (2018). An empirical examination of the development and impact of star power in major league baseball. *Journal of Sports Economics*, *19*(2), 155–187. doi:10.1177/1527002515626220

Littler, J. (2018). *Against meritocracy: Culture, power and myths of mobility.* Routledge.

Marshall, A. (1895). *Principles of economics.* Macmillan.

Mears, A. (2010). Size zero high-end ethnic: Cultural production and the reproduction of culture in fashion modeling. *Poetics*, *38*(1), 21–46. doi:10.1016/j.poetic.2009.10.002

Mears, A. (2011). *Pricing beauty: The making of a fashion model.* University of California Press.

Mijs, J. J. B. (2011). Van terecht onrecht naar pluriform talent. *Beleid En Maatschappij*, *38*(3), 327–333.

Mijs, J. J. B. (2016). The unfulfillable promise of meritocracy: Three lessons and their implications for justice in education. *Social Justice Research*, *29*(1), 14–34. doi:10.1007/s11211-014-0228-0

Mijs, J. J. B. (2019). The paradox of inequality: Income inequality and belief in meritocracy go hand in hand. *Socio-Economic Review*, *2019*, mwy051. doi:10.1093/ser/mwy051

Mincer, J. (1958). Investment in human capital and personal income distribution. *Journal of Political Economy*, *66*(4), 281–302. doi:10.1086/258055

Mittleman, J. (2018). A downward spiral? Childhood suspension and the path to juvenile arrest. *Sociology of Education*, *91*(3), 183–204. doi:10.1177/0038040718784603

Mulligan, T. (2018a). Do people deserve their economic rents? *Erasmus Journal for Philosophy and Economics*, *11*(2), 163–190. doi:10.23941/ejpe.v11i2.338

Mulligan, T. (2018b). *Justice and the meritocratic state.* Routledge.

Organisation for Economic Co-Operation and Development (OECD). (2008). *The* global competition for talent. Mobility of the highly skilled.

Pfeffer, F. T., & Killewald, A. (2018). Generations of advantage. Multigenerational correlations in family wealth. *Social Forces*, *96*(4), 1411–1442. doi:10.1093/sf/sox086

Piketty, T. (2014). *Capital in the twenty-first century.* Harvard University Press.

Prentice, D. A., & Carranza, E. (2002). What women and men should be, shouldn't be, are allowed to be, and don't have to be: The contents of prescriptive gender stereotypes. *Psychology of Women Quarterly*, *26*(4), 269–281. doi: 10.1111/1471-6402.t01-1-00066

Ricardo, D. (1817). *On the principles of political economy, and taxation.* J. Murray.

Rimfeld, K., Krapohl, E., Trzaskowski, M., Coleman, J. R. I., Selzam, S., Dale, P. S., Esko, T., Metspalu, A., & Plomin, R. (2018). Genetic influence on social outcomes during and after the Soviet era in Estonia. *Nature Human Behaviour*, *2*(4), 269–275. doi:10.1038/s41562-018-0332-5

Rosen, S. (1981). The economics of superstars. *The American Economic Review*, *71*(5), 845–858.

Schultz, T. W. (1960). Capital formation by education. *Journal of Political Economy*, *68*(6), 571–583. doi:10.1086/258393

Smeeding, T., Erikson, R., & Markus, J., (Eds.). (2011). *Persistence*, privilege, and parenting. The comparative study of intergenerational mobility. Russell Sage Foundation.

Sørensen, A. B. (1996). The structural basis of social inequality. *American Journal of Sociology*, *101*(5), 1333–1365. doi:10.1086/230825

Sørensen, A. B. (2000). Toward a sounder basis for class analysis. *American Journal of Sociology*, *105*(6), 1523–1558.

Tsay, A., Lamont, M., Abbott, A., & Guetzkow, J. (2003). From character to intellect: Changing conceptions of merit in the social sciences and humanities, 1951–1971. *Poetics*, *31*(1), 23–49. doi:10.1016/S0304-422X(03)00002-0

Van de Werfhorst, H. G., & Mijs, J. J. B. (2010). Achievement inequality and the institutional structure of educational systems: A comparative perspective. *Annual Review of Sociology*, *36*(1), 407–428. doi:10.1146/annurev.soc.012809.102538

Weeden, K. A., & Grusky, D. B. (2014). Inequality and market failure. *American Behavioral Scientist*, *58*(3), 473–491. doi:10.1177/0002764213503336

Welch, K., & Payne, A. A. (2018). Latino/a student threat and school disciplinary policies and practices. *Sociology of Education*, *91*(2), 91–110. doi:10.1177/0038040718757720

World Bank. (2010). *Talent abroad promoting growth and institutional development at home: Skilled diaspora as part of the country.*

Yamamoto, Y., & Brinton, M. C. (2010). Cultural capital in East Asian educational systems the case of Japan. *Sociology of Education*, *83*(1), 67–83. doi:10.1177/0038040709356567

The belief in innate talent and its implications for distributive justice

Mark C. Vopat

ABSTRACT
Although the commonly accepted view is that there are such things as natural talents, more than 20 years of research suggests the opposite. What passes for talented is attributable to a combination of social andenvironmental factors. If the current research on this topic holds true, then there are implications not only for various theories of distributive justice, but there are also serious implication for real world distributions. In this article I will argue that talent is not innate and that our belief in its innateness has serious theoretical and practical implications for distributive justice. Many of these implications can be seen in the ways resources and opportunities are distributed; particularly in the way they affect distributions to children.

Introduction

Perfect pitch (also known as absolute pitch) is the ability to pick out a note without reference to any other note. It is the ability to identify things like the fact that one's water glass vibrates at a perfect C# when tapped with a spoon; to play a single note on a piano and identify it without seeing the keyboard. As Will Crutchfield writes:

> Those who possess absolute pitch in its fullest manifestations can produce any note accurately on request and can unhesitatingly name the pitch or pitches of any pitched sound or group of sounds, all without reference to any previously sounded pitch. Implicit in this is a sense of each of the 12 notes of the chromatic scale as having a unique and particular character.[1]

This ability to identify a sound in this way is found in only 1 in 10,000 individuals. For many people this type of ability is an example of an innate ability; they are the natural talents or abilities that one is just born with, and which in many instances give the holder a leg up on others in certain fields. For example, Mozart, Stravinsky, and even Sinatra had it—which seems to indicate that it is a valuable trait to have in the music world.

Although an innate talent like perfect pitch is both impressive and valuable, it does raise certain moral concerns. The Mozarts, Monets, and Kasparovs seem to have talents others lack, and are much better situated to use them to take advantage of the rewards society attaches to these talents. What is also obvious is that these advantages are undeserved. It is not by any effort of their possessor that they have obtained some special ability (although they may work to develop it). On the standard account of natural ability, those that lack that talent cannot will it into existence.

Although the commonly accepted view is that there are such things as natural talents, more than 20 years of research suggests the opposite. What passes for talented is attributable to a combination of social and environmental factors. If what the findings of researchers such as K. Anders Ericson, and Benjamin Bloom holds true, then there are implications not only for various theories of distributive justice,[2] but there are also serious implication for real world distributions. Many of these implications can be seen in the ways resources and opportunities are distributed; particularly in the way they affect distributions to children.

In this article I will argue that talent is not innate and that our belief in its innateness has serious theoretical and practical implications for distributive justice. I begin with an examination of what we commonly view as talent, and why it is not innate. Next, I discuss some of the problems the rejection of innate talent has on the theories of justice proposes by John Rawls and Robert Nozick. Following this, I touch on some of the fundamentally unjust consequences that result in the areas of education and the formation of future citizens by relying on the idea of innate talent. Finally, I discuss some of the objections some might have to the rejection of innate talent.

1. What is innate talent?

Before discussing the problems with relying on the idea of innate talent, it is important to be clear what we mean by the term. We often refer to people as having a 'talent for business' or an 'ear for music'. We also refer to people as 'gifted' in this or that game or sport. While these colloquial expressions are fine for everyday use, they give the mistaken impression that one can be talented at nearly any activity. When discussing talent and whether it is in fact innate, it is necessary limit the types of activities to those that meet certain criteria. Not everything that we label as a talent can actually be objectively determined to be so.

First, to say that someone is talented in a particular area it is necessary that there is some way to measure their performance. For example, chess players can be ranked by the number of wins they have and the number of wins against those of greater or lesser ranking. Similarly, in a track and field event such as the long jump, athletes can easily be ranked by the distance they traverse. A second feature of talent is that it is by its nature competitive. Talents are things that can be stacked up against one another. They are features that express themselves when compared with others. If I desire to know who is an expert in a field, direct competition is the best way to settle the issue. A third feature of talent is that it is generally associated with an established body of knowledge. For example, in chess there is an extensive list of opening moves. The chess master or grandmaster is able to recognize a number of these standard openings and execute the strategically best response. Talent therefore consists partially of an ability to recall and apply a well-established body of knowledge. Finally, what is common to most talents is the existence of teachers or coaches that are able to help others develop their talents. These coaches are able to develop training regimes that progressively develop the innate ability of the talented individual. When we speak of talented or gifted athletes, we can also point to coaches or trainers that have themselves already obtained some proficiency in the activity, or have at least studied and developed effective training regimes.[3]

Talent is thus characterized by its measurability, competitiveness, an established body of knowledge and the existence of teachers or coaches. These provide the sufficient conditions for the recognition of a skill in which one can be deemed talented. Noticeably absent from this list is any mention of some identifiable biological or genetic element of talent. In study after study, genius, talent, expertise—whatever name we want to give it—consistently proves to be an elusive biological trait. Even in families that seem to produce more talented individuals, researchers have shown that the environment in which the child was raised accounts for his or her ability, and not the genetic pool from which they came.[4] As I have discussed elsewhere,[5] studies of world class concert pianists, accomplished sculptors, Olympic swimmers, world class tennis players, mathematicians, and neurologists have shown that the initial natural talent attributed to individuals across disciplines had very little if anything to do with their successes later in life. As Bloom writes:

> Our present findings point to the conclusion that exceptional levels of talent development requires certain types of environmental support, special experiences, excellent teaching, and appropriate motivational encouragement at each stage of development. No matter what the quality of the initial gifts, each of the individuals we studied went through many years of special development under the care of attentive parents and the tutelage and supervision of a remarkable series of teachers and coaches.[6]

Numerous other studies have also failed to find evidence for anything like natural talents or abilities as the basis for later success in a given occupation or field. The striking lack of correlation between success and natural talents has led researchers to look more closely at the environment of exceptional individuals—and it is here that they find a plausible explanation for why some individuals become accomplished and other do not.[7]

Accounting for natural talent

How do we account for innate talent? It turns out the answer is fairly simple. Children that exhibit the most 'talent' are those which have had the most training and practice. But it is not just practice that leads to exceptional ability. The type of practice—what Anders Ericsson has termed deliberate practice—is where we find our explanation.

There are five key components to deliberate practice. First, deliberate practice requires oversight by teachers that understand how abilities can be developed. Second, deliberate practice requires that one be taken outside of his or her comfort zone. Third, achieving excellence requires setting a specific goal and a plan to achieve those goals. Fourth, it requires full attention and conscious action. Finally, deliberate practice to achieve excellence depends on effective mental representations. Mental representations are 'preexisting patterns of information — facts, images, rules relationships, and so on — that are held in long-term memory and that can be used to respond quickly and effectively in certain types of situations.'[8]

There are two additional aspects of deliberate practice, particularly when applied to children. First, deliberate practice on the part of children requires discipline that is normally instilled by parents. Children aren't born with the type of discipline required for deliberate practice, but develop it over time and with support from others. A child's engaging in a particular activity is dependent upon the encouragement and later the support of his or her parents. Without the initial push from someone else, the child is unlikely to have taken an interest in, or had the resources to continue in an activity. This leads to the second aspect, namely, deliberate practice requires support over an extended period of time. So while intense training is important, equally important is family support. A single instance of encouragement is not enough, as the development of an ability takes place after an extend period of practice. What follow from this is that children with less exposure, fewer opportunities, and limited support are less likely to achieve the same levels of expertise as other more fortunate children.[9]

2. Problems for traditional theories of justice

The idea that innate ability, or talent is not natural, but can be taught expands our conception of what human beings are capable of if given appropriate support. It also poses a challenge to various social structures that have been premised upon the idea that some people are just gifted. If anyone with enough dedication, can achieve superior ability in nearly any area, then greater attention must be paid to why some have this opportunity and others don't. It also has profound implications for many theories of distributive justice. Two theories that loom large in the political canon, both on their own and because of their influence on subsequent theorists, are those of John Rawls and Robert Nozick. Both Rawls and Nozick hold the common view that talent is somehow innate, though they differ on how this fact should or should not effect distributive shares. In the sections that follow, I offer a sketch of the ways in which the rejection of innate talent has substantive implications for each of their respective theories.

John Rawls

In *A Theory of Justice*[10], John Rawls addresses the issue of natural talents and their affect on justice. For Rawls, natural talent cannot serve as the basis for a theory of distributive justice. In fact, Rawls argues that the unjust affects that natural talents have on our current distribution of goods is already observable:

> The existing distribution of income and wealth, say, is the cumulative effect of prior distributions of natural assets—that is, natural talents and abilities—as these have been developed or left unrealized, and their use favored or disfavored over time by social circumstances and such chance contingencies as accident and good fortune. Intuitively, the most obvious injustice of the system of natural liberty is that it permits distributive shares to be improperly influenced by these factors so arbitrary from a moral point of view[11]

For Rawls, because no one deserves their natural talents anymore than one deserves the lack of talents; their distribution is as he says 'arbitrary from a moral point of view'. These talents give some individuals greater life chances than others. Further, he recognizes that even amongst individuals with the same natural talent there is likely to be substantial inequality because of their arbitrary starting points in life. Children with equal talent are likely to have unequal prospects when some are born into social and familial situations in which their talent cannot develop. As Rawls writes:

> The extent to which natural capacities develop and reach fruition is affected by all kinds of social conditions and class attitudes. Even the willingness to make an effort, to try, and so to be deserving in the ordinary sense is itself dependent upon happy family and social circumstances. It is impossible in practice to secure equal chances of achievement and culture for those similarly endowed, and therefore we may want to adopt a principle which recognizes this fact and also mitigates the arbitrary effects of the natural lottery itself.[12]

Rawls's response to the impact natural talents can have on distributive justice is to introduce the 'difference principle'. The difference principle holds that some inequalities are allowed provided they are to the advantage of the least well off members of society. This principle is acceptable to the people in Rawls's original position because it both allows and encourages individuals to develop their natural talents and abilities, as well as provides an added social benefit; those that lack these natural talents get some benefits from these natural inequalities. Since these are 'natural' and not subject to social distribution, this essentially treats natural talents as a social good—something distributed to all.

This approach to natural talent has an intuitive appeal. If talent isn't something we can distribute, then it is unfair that some people who arbitrarily are born with certain abilities should be able to disproportionately benefit from them. If I didn't deserve to not have a particular ability (or for that matter any special ability), then why should other who didn't deserve to have a particular ability be able to enjoy greater social goods? Furthermore, the talents one has that provide these extra benefits are often socially relative. For example, the ability to throw a ball through a hoop is only valuable in societies that value basketball. The same talent for hand-eye coordination may not benefit one in a society that values kicking a ball into a net.

Rawls's difference principle, and the intuitive argument itself hinges on the idea that talent is innate, and that some people are naturally disadvantaged. If talent isn't innate, then this poses a problem for Rawls. While there may still be naturally disadvantaged people (e.g. the developmentally disabled or a person with a physical disability), once we remove the idea that talent is innate the vast majority of the least well-of are only so because of some structural deficiency. As such, the difference principle goes from being a corrective on the effect of traits beyond our control, to a way of maintaining an unequal and possibly unjust social arrangements. After all, with the right support, the vast majority of children can achieve what we would have considered only possible by those with exceptional ability.

Robert Nozick

While Rawls's theory attempts to correct the a affects that natural talents may have on distributive shares, Nozick's theory makes no apologies for the resulting distributions. A distribution is only problematic if it results from an exchange that violates the principles of his entitlement theory[13].

The entitlement theory consists of three principles that determine our justice in holdings. Nozick prefers the term 'holdings' to 'distribution' as the latter implies that there is some person or mechanism that distributes things. His theory attempts to offer an account of when one can legitimately claim to justly hold the goods they have. To claim that I am entitled to the goods that I have entails that I acquired them in certain ways. The first way I may acquire is according to the principle of just initial acquisition; an account of how we come to own some previously unowned thing. The second way I am entitled to some good is if it is in accord with the principle of transfer; an account of when a transfer between individuals is legitimate. Finally, there is the principle of the rectification of injustice which covers situations in which a holding is the result of a violation of the previous two principles. Nozick states these principles as follows:

1. A person who acquires a holding in accordance with the principle of justice in acquisition is entitled to that holding.
2. A person who acquires a holding in accordance with the principle of justice in transfer, from someone else entitled to the holding, is entitled to the holding.
3. No one is entitled to a holding except by (repeated) applications of 1 and 2.[14]

Since all acquisitions cannot be the result of previous acquisitions (else we would be faced with an infinite regress of exchanges), Nozick embraces a Lockean conception of initial acquisition. Assuming there is some unowned thing, the mixing of one's labor with that thing makes it one's property. And this property right is absolute; taking it for any purpose without the owner's permission is an illegitimate transfer.

One of the appeals of Nozick's approach is its simplicity. Social distributions are the result of individual, voluntary exchanges. Assuming that my initial acquisition was just, then all subsequent transactions are also just. The principles of acquisition and exchange make speedy work of the issue of natural talents and abilities. If a talent is something that I possess, and that possession was not obtained illegitimately (e.g. through force or fraud), then I am entitled to it and any benefits it may confer on me. As Nozick writes:

> It is not true, for example, that a person earns Y (a right to keep a painting he's made, praise for writing *A Theory of Justice* and so on) only if he's earned (or otherwise deserves) whatever he used (including natural assets) in the process of earning Y. Some of the things he uses he just may have, not illegitimately. It needn't be that the foundations underlying desert are themselves deserved, all the way down.[15]

Much like Rawls, the assumption Nozick makes is that natural talents are beyond our control. Since they can't be distributed they are simply things we have and are thus legitimate holdings. But, if talents aren't innate, then they are the result of access to previously distributed goods. For example, those that exchange their musical talent for money, must have had access to resources to develop those abilities. Consequently, it becomes an open question as to whether those that have acquired these 'talents' did so with resources that were legitimately acquired.

It seems clear that given the magnitude of past injustices based on things such as race, sex, sexual orientation, and socio-economic status, it is difficult to believe that there isn't something at least partially unjust in some previous transfers. For example, African Americans make up approximately 1.8%, and Hispanics 2.4% of orchestra members in the United States, while comprising 13.4% and 18.1% of the population respectively.[16] It seems highly unlikely that the lack of minority representation in orchestras is because minorities don't like formal music. When we remove the idea of innate talent and replace it with dedicated practice it is more likely that the socially disadvantaged lack of exposure, resources, support, and coaching accounts for this racial disparity.

Conclusions

Both liberal and libertarian views presuppose the existence of natural talents. Once this presumption is removed—and possibly replaced with deliberate practice—a re-evaluation of their central principles is required. A Rawlsian liberal can no longer rely on the difference principle as a means of addressing natural inequalities. While the principle may still apply to some in society (for example those with severe physical or mental impairment) the set of individuals to which it would be applied is now substantially circumscribed. Since society can in essence distribute talent, I would suggest that Rawls's theory needs to re-examine the roles played by several social institutions in the distribution of resources. It would also seem that institutions such as those of the family would take on a new significance in social and political theorizing. Similarly, institutions that were once considered a matter of local concern, for example, the control and funding of public schools, may need to be re-evaluated on a societal level.

The libertarian does not fair much better than the Rawlsian. Although Nozick's theory does not find it necessary to address the acquisition of legitimately acquired goods, talents themselves now need to be scrutinized to determine whether they were in essence ill-gotten gains. If the primary reason someone has exceptional artistic ability is because of the resources his or her parents were able to invest in their training, and those resources were acquired (even in part) from an illegitimate acquisition, then the talent itself is now suspect. Nozick's theory was already questionable on these grounds, but now they become even more pressing in light of the rejection of innate talent.

3. Additional consequences of believing in innate talent

Just as the rejection of innate talent has consequences for theories of distributive justice, it also has consequences for real world distributions. In particular, I will examine some of the ways that the rejection of innate talent affects individuals—particularly children—as well as society as a whole. In what follows I begin by examining how innate talent leads to unequal access to educational resources. Next I will examine how the idea of a child's right to an open future is affected by presupposing the existence of gifted and non-gifted children. Finally, I will look at the broader consequences this belief has on the formation of future citizens.

Liberal approach

Before proceeding to an examination of the various deleterious consequences of innate talent, a few clarifications are in order. The arguments that I will be making presuppose a liberal understanding of our individual obligations to children, an obligation that I assume is shared by the wider moral community. It is against this backdrop that I argue the belief in innate talents results in a moral failure to children, along with a wider harm to society in general.

The moral community that will be assumed here is the standard liberal society. Although there are a number of different theories that claim to be liberal, they all share certain general features. In the 'The Common Faith of Liberalism,'[17] Jean Hampton argues that there are five major commitments common to all liberal traditions. For my purposes here I will focus on three that I believe are relevant to determining children's interests:

1. A commitment to the idea that people in a political society must be free.
2. A commitment to equality of the people in the political society.
3. A commitment to the idea that the state's role must be defined such that it enhances the freedom and equality of the people.

3a. The state has the best chance of securing the freedom and equality of it citizens when it is organized as a democracy.

3b. The state can only insure freedom by pursuing policies that implement toleration and freedom of conscience for all citizens.

3c. The state must stay out of the individual's construction of his own life plans-his 'conception of the good'.[18]

Although I may not know which conception of the good life a child may eventually come to endorse, I do recognize that within the liberal framework it is up to the child to choose amongst the various options open to him or her. Since the liberal society ought to guarantee equality of its members, it is the responsibility of both parents and society to ensure that children are not disadvantaged in their ability to choose among these competing conceptions. The conceptions of the good open to any particular child should be a function of his or her effort coupled with the basic goods necessary for realizing that conception, and should not be dependent on the arbitrary starting point afforded by his or her birth. And it is here that education plays a pivotal role in the future autonomy of the child.

It is through education, and particularly through a robust educational system that children can realize and develop their interests and abilities. It is also through knowledge of competing conceptions of the good life that children begin the process of self-actualization that is essential to their living a life in line with their own personal conception of the good. Additionally, education provides the child with the tools that will be necessary later in life to revise his or her conception of the good life. While some people may settle on a particular way of life at a relatively young age, many individuals find the need to try out various ways of living before finding the one that is right for them.[19] The importance of education in the autonomy, equality, and self-actualization of the child supports the view that restricting a child's education on the basis of natural talent is a fundamental violation of a child's rights.

Unequal access to resources

One area where the belief in innate talent has had a deleterious impact is in the area of education. Many of our educational institutions are implicitly premised on the idea that certain children are simply more naturally gifted than others. Once this assumption has been made, it is easy to rationalize treating some children differently than others. If a child has a 'gift' for music, then providing that child with the additional resources to develop that talent appears morally unproblematic. After all, a non-gifted child will not be able to take advantage of the additional resources; they would in essence be wasted on the non-gifted student.

As I have written elsewhere[20], this idea that some students are naturally talented has been the impetus for the establishment of selective magnet schools.[21] Selective or competitive magnet schools require some form of entrance exam, audition or portfolio in order to be accepted. The focus of these schools is to give the best students educational opportunities they could not obtain in their home school. The basis for this differential treatment are the talents and the abilities these students demonstrate. In such instances, this differential treatment is justified on the grounds that though we may not be treating all students equally, equality doesn't demand that we waste resources on those that lack the talent or ability take advantage of the opportunities provided to them.

There are several respects in which these selective magnet school negatively impact children. First, they siphon off resources from other schools. Selective magnet schools often require additional resources to staff their speciality programs, and these resources are often at the expense of 'regular' schools. Additionally, these schools also provide what Adam Swift has termed *relative* and *absolute* advantages to some students, and relative and absolute disadvantages to others. Relative disadvantage occurs when a good for one individual comes at the expense of another. Students that are provided with greater educational resources; more competent instructors; along with additional deliberate practice, are more likely to advance in their chosen areas of study. This advantage tends to compound itself as the students moves up the educational ladder from selective grade school all the way to selective University; which ultimately culminates in greater economic opportunities later in life relative to his or her peers[22].

A similar situation arises in the case of absolute disadvantage. Absolute disadvantage is the loss experienced by those that are left behind. It is no surprise that the parents that take advantage of magnet schools are also parents that aregenerally more highly educated, engaged, and socio-economically advantaged. Similarly, the children of such parents are 'more likely to have been socialized into aspirations, skill and attitudes conducive to educational success'.[23] Their move to selective magnet schools has a negative impact on the peer environment that remains. The students not at the magnet schools do not get the advantages of being influenced by these students.

Although it may appear that the issue of talent in education only applies to magnet schools, its affects have become more far reaching. Many non-magnet public schools have taken a page from the magnet school approach and created their own internal 'gifted and talented' programs.[24] Rather than remove children entirely from their home school, these programs identify gifted students and reassign them to classes with other identified students. While some socialization occurs between the gifted and non-gifted students, the gifted classes often follow a more challenging and robust curriculum. This sets up those students lucky enough to be selected for these programs to benefit in many of the ways outlined above. So, magnet schools are not the only instance of talent interfering with access to resources; many traditional schools are also redistributing on the specious foundation of innate talent.[25]

Open future

The preceding sections have noted the problems with the idea of innate talent on a practical level. But there is an additional moral aspect, namely a child's right to an open future.[26] While children do not have the complex commitments or interests of adults, it is reasonable to assume that they will eventually have an interest in exploring or pursuing certain life goals. This interest will necessitates their being provided certain resources, or what Rawls refers to as primary goods. For example, all children require food, clothing, shelter, emotional support, and protection from a sometime dangerous world. In addition to these goods, it is reasonable to assume that children will eventually develop, or wish to develop their own conception of the good life. Though we do not know what conception they will ultimately embrace, we do recognize that they will require additional sorts of goods to pursue that conception. The belief in innate ideas limits the opportunity, encouragement, and deliberate practice necessary for a child to achieve his or her chosen life goals.

Within the liberal framework it is up to the child to choose amongst the various options open to him or her. Since the liberal society ought to guarantee equality of its members, it is the responsibility of both parents and society to ensure that children are not disadvantaged in their ability to choose among these competing conceptions. The conceptions of the good open to any particular child should be a function of his or her willingness to put in the time and effort necessary to develop their expertise in a given area, and not on the questionable basis of innate talent.

It is through education, and particularly through a robust educational system that children can realize and develop their interests and abilities. Education provides the child with the tools that will be necessary later in life to revise his or her conception of the good life.

The importance of education in the autonomy, equality, and self-actualization of the child supports the view that restricting a child's education opportunities on the grounds of innate talent violates the fundamental liberal commitments to children. For example, if each child is entitled to choose there own conception of the good life, then restricting their educational opportunities in music, art, or engineering, results in a number of life options are closed off to them. Such restrictions constitute a violation of their fundamental rights as members of the moral community. A system of education that relies on the idea of innate talent or the gifted does just this.[27]

Social consequences

The belief in innate talent has a negative impact on the formation of an educated citizenry. This impact is really the cumulative effect of the problems discussed in the previous sections.

Once you accept innate talent the natural response is to separates students into those that will benefit from additional resources and those who won't. Those that are deemed gifted are either encouraged to attend magnet schools, or moved into special programs within their home school. The question that remains is what is done with the rest of the students?

Responses to this question have varied from school district to school district. In some cases students are provided a general education and left to their own devices after high school. In other cases, students are encouraged to enter career programs to prepare them for occupations that do not require college or the extensive training found in music or the arts. But in nearly all cases the curriculum for those that are not considered gifted focuses on the applicability of education to the economic well-being of the child.

Focussing on economic well-being would not be problematic if the purpose of education generally was to create new workers. Clearly though education— particularly public education— was meant to do more than provide a pipeline from childhood to worker. From the time of the founding fathers education was touted as a means of encouraging and protecting democracy. As Thomas Jefferson wrote in a letter to George Wyeth:

> I think by far the most important bill in our whole code is that for the diffusion of knowledge among the people. No other sure foundation can be devised for the preservation of freedom, and happiness.[28]

The idea that education is about more than preparation for economic independence (though that can be one aspect of its purpose) fits nicely with the idea that children should be able to choose their own conception of the good life. The ability to choose one's conception of the good life presupposes the existence of a stable democratic society that protects the rights of its citizens. An educated citizenry is a necessary part of that stable society. So while there may be a number of positive economic externalities from education, we cannot forget the important civic role it plays in children's lives.

The affect education has on civic engagement is not merely speculative. The more education an individual receives the, the more likely they are to be civically engaged. As Thomas Dee notes in his study of the effects of additional schooling:

> The results of these evaluations suggest that additional schooling, both at the secondary and post-secondary levels, had large and statistically significant effects on voter participation. I also find that the

> additional secondary schooling significantly increase the frequency of newspaper readership as well as the amount of support for allowing most forms of possibly controversial free speech.[29]

It is worth noting that vocational, trade, and business school students were not included under the definition of post-secondary education[30]. It is also important to note that junior, community and 4-year university requirements are substantively different than what are found in trade and vocational schools, for example, general education courses in the humanities and social sciences.

These results have been noted in other studies as well. In examining the connection between education and improved citizenship in both the United States and the United Kingdom, Milligan, Moretti and Oreopoulis found that:

> Overall, our results for the United States lend support to the argument that education generates positive externalities in the form of enhanced political behavior. Our findings indicate that education benefits a representative democracy both by increasing the quantity of citizens' involvement in the electoral process (increased probability of voting) as well as the quality of their involvement (increased information on candidates and political parties).[31]

This conclusion bring us full circle to the problem with innate talent. When we accept the idea that some individuals are more gifted than others, our concern is not to promote excellence; rather, is to provide some basic level of competency. The concern focusses on ensuring that the exceptional have the resources to flourish; while everyone else is employable. This approach is problematic for at least two reasons: first, it limits the choice that individuals have; secondly, it introduces a purely instrumental aspect to education. As the studies above note, the types of education that make for a better, more informed citizen is not what is typically found in trade or career training.

The repercussions of believing in innate talent has far reaching implications. You remove certain resources from a large number of students, which simultaneously limits their choices and adversely affects there preparedness for informed citizenship. Similarly, the inadvertent use of deliberate practice in career orientated education makes it highly likely that students will show a talent for one career path over another, not because of any innate talent, but because they have been primed for a particular career path. This aspect of programs such as career academies raise serious questions about the influence that business has on education, as well as the more fundamental questions about the nature of choice and who has the right to choose or influence the choices children make.

4. Objections

The implications for recognizing that talent is not innate is not without controversy. First, there are those unwilling to accept the idea that there really aren't people who are naturally gifted. The introduction to this article presented the example of perfect pitch as an innate ability. Although perfect pitch is observed in a very small number of people, it turns out that even that trait can be learned. Psychologist Ayako Sakakibara put twenty-four students between the ages of two and six through a training course designed to identify simple chords on a piano. Through deliberate practice a group of music students at the Ichionkai Music School in Tokyo were able to acquire the ability in a year and a half:

> The children were given four or five short training sessions per day, each lasting just a few minutes, and each child continued training until he or she could identify all fourteen of the target chords that Sakakibara had selected. Some of the children completed the training in less tha a year, while others took as long as a year and a half... After completing training every one of the children in the study had developed perfect pitch and could identify individual notes played on the piano.[32]

There are numerous other examples of abilities that seem extraordinary but are actually the result of deliberate practice. Providing a full blown defense against every example the skeptic of the non-existence innate talent can think of is beyond the scope of this article; though there are three specific objections that are worth a brief discussion. The first is the role of IQ in talent; the second is the issue of physical differences; the third the role that family or upbringing may play in how we socially address talent.

Intelligence

It is commonly assumed that talent is linked in some way to intelligence or IQ. A talented mathematician or musician is often thought to have abilities that extend to other areas of expert performance. Unfortunately for the aspiring polymath, it turns out that talent in one area doesn't translate into exceptional ability in another. Since the training needed to achieve superior ability requires deliberate practice over many years, there are few people that have the time, resources, or discipline to focus on more than one area of specialization.

If IQ is not a predictor of talent, then what does it predict? According to Ericson, although there is some disagreement about what IQ tests actually measure, he believes it is best to view them as what they have been shown to predict:

> IQ is best thought of not as innate intelligence but rather simply as what IQ tests measure, which can include such things as knowledge about relatively rare words and aquired skills in mathematics. Without delving deeply into the debate, I will just say that I think it is best to not equate IQ with innate intelligence but simply to stick with the facts and think of IQ as some cognitive factor, measured by IQ tests, that has been shown to predict certain things, such as success in school[33]

The lack of correlation between IQ and superior performance has been the focus of numerous studies. In each instance IQ has little if anything to do with excellence, and in the case of elite chess players, it turns out that *lower* IQ players were slightly better players:

> Among these twenty-three elite players the amount of practice was still the major factor determining their chess skills, but intelligence played no noticeable role. While the elite group did have somewhat higher average IQ than the average IQ for the entire group of fifty-seven, the players in the elite group with lower IQs were, on average, slightly better players than those in the elite group with higher IQs.[34]

Similar examples can be given in disciplines such as physics, biology, and engineering. While many scientists have IQ scores that are above average, several Noble Laureates have scores below the 132 required to get them into Mensa.[35]

Physical limitations

There is no doubt that certain physical characteristics can privilege or limit the opportunities of children. The average height of an NBA basketball player is 6'7"[36], while the average height of a man in the United States is 5'9"[37]. Clearly, one cannot deliberately practice his or he way to greater height. Still, there have been three players in the NBA who have been shorter than the national average: Spud Webb at 5'7"; Earl Boykins at 5'5"; Muggsy Boques at 5'3"[38].

While physical characteristics can limit opportunities, notice that these are not limitations of talent. As was noted in the example of shorter than average NBA players, even the disadvantages associated with height can be overcome with enough skill and practice. It is also important to note two other aspects of physical limitations. First, having a physical characteristic is not the same as having a talent or skill. There are many tall individuals that cannot play basketball well. Being a good or excellent player is not equivalent to having a particular characteristic. Secondly, athletic competitions themselves define and or presuppose the normal range of functioning required in order to engage in the sport. They also define the equipment that can be used. If you change any of these assumptions then what defines excellence also changes. For example, if basketball was played from a seated position—say in a wheelchair—it is likely that many NBA players would not excel in the sport as they do now.[39]

Family background

As was mentioned in the discussion of the relationship between excellence and deliberate practice, family support is essential to success. It was also noted that there does not appear to be any genetic aspect to talent. Still, there may be aspects of family and possibly even genetics that might make it more likely that some will achieve excellence in a way that makes it appear some innate factor is at work. For example, it seems that some people have the focus, determination, endurance, or grit that others seem to lack. Is this trait something that can be attributed wholly to one's upbringing? Simply making resources available, and even actively encouraging children in some pursuit does not guarantee that they will attain excellence.

A related question is whether one's interest in some pursuit is itself somehow hardwired into some individuals. While the talent for something may not be innate, is it possible that there is something in the make-up of certain individuals that makes some pursuits more attractive than others? For example, why is it that some people are moved by music, while others are attracted to mathematics? Is is possible that families that produce multiple generations of writers or actors just happen to have some mental characteristic that makes those pursuits more appealing? As Erisson has noted:

> I suspect that such genetic differences—if they exist—are most likely to manifest themselves through the necessary practice and efforts that go into developing a skill. Perhaps, for example, some children are born with a suite of genes that cause them to get more pleasure from drawing or from making music than other children. Then those children will be more likely to draw or to make music than other children. If they're put in art classes or music classes, they're more likely to spend more time practicing because it is more fun for them.[40]

Regardless of whether certain individuals *naturally* find certain activities more pleasing than others, our goal should be that everyone, particularly the children in our care, have the opportunity to discover those things that appeal to them.

5. Conclusion

The belief that some individuals are naturally talented, while others are not has serious implications that have generally gone ignored in the philosophic literature. In these articles, I have only scratched the surface of the problems this belief has had on distributive justice, education, and society as a whole. Even this brief account raises questions about the fairness of many of our educational practices, and the effects they may have on future generations. Who know how many exceptional authors, artists, mathematicians, and physicists, we have lost to the specious idea of innate talent.

Notes

1. Crutchfield, Will "Classical Music: There May Be More to Music Than Meets A Typical Ear" *New York Times,* https://www.nytimes.com/1990/12/23/arts/classical-music-there-may-be-more-to-music-than-meets-a-typical-ear.html
2. Some of these theoretical implications will be addressed in section 4.
3. Anders Ericsson and Robert Pool, *Peak: Secrets from the New Science of Expertise* (Boston: Houghton Mifflin Harcourt 2006), 85–86.
4. In Developing Talent in Young People, a group of researchers led by Benjamin Bloom studied individuals that by all accounts would be considered exceptional in their respective fields see Benjamin S. Bloom ed. *Developing Talent in Young People* (New York: Ballantine Books 1985).
5. Mark C. Vopat, "School Uniforms and Freedom of Expression" *Ethics and Education* Vol. 5 No. 3 (November 2010).
6. Benjamin S. Bloom ed. *Developing Talent in Young People* (New York: Ballantine Books 1985), 543.
7. *The Cambridge Handbook of Expertise and Expert Performance* ed. K. Anders Ericsson, Neil Charness, Paul J. Feltovich and Robert R. Hoffman (Cambridge: Cambridge University Press, 2006) Similar findings appear in

other studies of genius or exceptional talent. In *Genius Explained,* Michael J. A. Howe argues that individuals from Darwin to Einstein were not born exceptional, but developed those traits people would later attribute to genius.

8. Anders Ericsson and Robert Pool, *Peak: Secrets from the New Science of Expertise* (Boston: Houghton Mifflin Harcourt, 2006), p. 65–66.
9. K. Anders Ericsson, Michael J. Prietula, and Edward T. Cokely, "The Making of an Expert" in *Harvard Business Review:Managing for the Long Term* July-August 2007 pp. 1–7.
10. John Rawls, *A Theory of Justice revised edition.* (Cambridge: Belknap/Harvard University Press, 1971).
11. Ibid., 63.
12. Ibid., 64.
13. Robert Nozick, *Anarchy, State, and Utopia* (Oxford: Blackwell Books Inc., 1999).
14. Ibid., 151.
15. Ibid., 225.
16. https://americanorchestras.org/images/stories/diversity/Racial-Ethnic-and-Gender-Diversity-in-the-Orchestra-Field-Final-92116.pdf

    https://www.census.gov/quickfacts/fact/table/US/PST045218
17. Jean Hampton, "The Common Faith of Liberalism," Pacific Philosophical Quarterly 75 (1994): 186–216.
18. Ibid., 191–193. The features not considered include: "4. Any political society must be justified to the individuals within it, if that society is to be legitimate. (Justified by reason) 5. Reason is the tool by which the liberal state governs. Whatever the religious, moral or metaphysical views of the people, they are expected to deal with one another in the political arena through rational argument and reasonable attitude, and the legitimating arguments directing at individuals in order procure their consent must be based on reason."
19. There are of course limitations that can be legitimately placed on the number of liberal good lives open to an individual. Obviously, those that violate moral or legally justified rules (assuming they are just laws) are not viable options. Also, those choices that may be options when the child is a fully autonomous adult, may be discouraged while the child is still a probationary member of society. For example, living as a functional alcoholic may be an option for an adult member of society, but such a life may be left off the list as of viable options presented to children.
20. Mark Vopat, "Magnet Schools, Innate Talent and Social Justice" Volume: 9 issue: 1, page(s): 59–72.

    Article first published online: March 21, 2011; Issue published: March 1, 2011.
21. There are currently 3,176 magnet schools in the U.S. serving 2.52 million students serving more total students than the 5,772 charter schools also found in school districts across the country. See Morgan Polikoff and Tenice Hardaway, "Don't forget magnet schools when thinking about school choice" *Brookings*, Thursday, March 16, 2017, accessed February 13, 2020, https://www.brookings.edu/research/dont-forget-magnet-schools-when-thinking-about-school-choice/.
22. Adam Swift, "The Morality of School Choice" *Theory and Research in Education* Vol. 2(1) (2004).
23. Ibid., 11.
24. See for example the programs found in the Akron Public Schools https://www.akronschools.com/departments/teaching_and_learning/gifted_and_talented; and the Metro Nashville Public Schools https://www.mnps.org/academies-of-nashville/ (Both sites last accessed 2019-01-10).
25. In a study done by the National Association for Gifted Children and the Council of State Directors of Programs for the Gifted 32 out of 40 states had some type of state level mandate on identifying and serving gifted children. See Andy Smarick "The Contradiction at the Heart of Public Education", October 10, 2019, accessed February 18, 2020, https://www.theatlantic.com/ideas/archive/2019/10/gifted-and-talented-programs-arent-problem/599752/.
26. Joel Feinberg, "Child's Right to an Open Future" *in Whose Child* (Totowa: Littlefield, 1980).
27. According to Whitney Pirtle, gifted and talented programs have a serious racial equality problem. While 17% of the population is black; less than 10% of black students are part of gifted and talented programs. On the other hand 53% of remedial students are black. See "The Other Segregation" *The Atlantic* April 23, 2019, accessed February 18, 2020, https://www.theatlantic.com/education/archive/2019/04/gifted-and-talented-programs-separate-students-race/587614/
28. Andrew Lipscomb and Albert Bergh, eds. *The Writings of Thomas Jefferson* 20 Volumes (Washington D.C. : 1903–1904), 5:396.
29. Thomas S. Dee, "Are There Civic Returns to Education?" *Journal of Public Economics* 88 (2004) 1699.
30. College entrance is defined by Dee as enrollment in a junior, community, or four year college.
31. Kevin Mulligan, Enrico Moretti, Philip Oreopoulos, "Does Education Improve Citizenship? Evidence from the United States and the United Kingdom." *Journal of Public Economics* 88 (2004) 1670.
32. Ericsson and Poole, xiv–xv.
33. Ericsson and Poole 227.
34. Ibid., 231.

35. Ibid., 234.
36. National Basketball Association website http://www.nba.com/article/2018/10/24/takeaways-2018-19-nba-roster-survey (Last accessed 2019-01-10).
37. Center for Disease Control and Prevention https://www.cdc.gov/nchs/fastats/body-measurements.htm (Last accessed 2019-01-10).
38. Wikipedia, "List of shortest players in National Basketball Association history" https://en.wikipedia.org/wiki/List_of_shortest_players_in_National_Basketball_Association_history (Last accessed 2019-01-10).
39. Another example where a slight change in rules or equipment changes who excels is the case of softball pitcher Jennie Finch who was able to strikeout professional baseball players such as Alex Rodriguez, Albert Pujols and Barry Bonds. ESPN "After 14 years, Jennie Finch finally gets her revenge on Sean Casey" http://www.espn.com/espnw/culture/the-buzz/article/19551928/after-14-years-jennie-finch-gets-revenge-sean-casey (Last accessed 2019-01-10).
40. Ericsson and Poole, 237.

Disclosure statement

No potential conflict of interest was reported by the author.

A limited defense of talent as a criterion for access to educational opportunities

Winston C. Thompson 

ABSTRACT
In recent work, Joseph Fishkin has helpfully enriched understandings of equality of opportunity as a feature of distributive justice schemes. One branch of his argument focuses upon the degree to which 'merit', as a function of talent and effort, is conceptually and practically vexing for these goals. While Thompson is in general agreement with the direction of Fishkin's critiques and new offerings, in this article he extends and strengthens Fishkin's analysis of talent, specifically focusing upon its role as a defensible criterion for access to developmentally useful educational opportunities.
Developing an account sympathetic to Fishkin's contributions, Thompson provides a limited defense of talent as a morally relevant criterion for access to some educational opportunities. Of course, Thompson acknowledges that this relevance is not absolute and, therefore, points towards reasons why talent enjoys only this occasionally relevant status in relation to educational opportunities and what systemic issues ought to be avoided as a result.

1. Introduction

Lay and popular principled conceptual orientations towards talent as a criterion for access to educational opportunities accept its usage in a number of contexts (Kotzee & Martin, 2013; Merisotis, 2015; Wolff & Wolff, 2005). That view has been challenged by a wave of recent work that aims to resist the status quo acceptance of talent's role in the distribution of these opportunities (Bailey, 2007; Beckwith, 1999; Elford, 2016; Petrović, 2009; Slote, 2013; Vopat, 2011). These critiques offer important and necessary arguments regarding the undesirability of talent as a criterion for access to educational opportunities. Still, might a limited defense of talent be advanced while nonetheless embracing the core insights of these critical works?

This article aims to offer such a defense by focusing upon supporting arguments within one source of potential criticism of traditional understandings of talent's role in the equal distribution of educational opportunities, Joseph's Fishkin's *Bottlenecks: A New Theory of Equality of Opportunity* (2014). Fishkin provides a focused view (rather than a full theory) of egalitarian distributive justice that might serve as a productive entry to careful consideration of talent and educational opportunity.

Engaging with this work, this article makes a modest claim (with wide ramifications for further analysis): despite good evidence that many egalitarian schemes of distributive justice (as applied to educational opportunity) that depend, in part, upon conceptions of natural talent have been shown to be meaningfully flawed, a cautious defense of talent as a criterion (herein understood as significantly contributory portion of an evaluative standard rather than as a sole determinant of an outcome) for equal access to developmentally useful educational opportunities can be made. In this, the article specifically addresses talent's essential role as a criterion for determining developmental usefulness, potentially in the service of broader equality-informed distributive aims.[1]

While this paper is in general agreement with the direction of Fishkin's critiques and new offerings, it aims to extend and strengthen his analysis of talent, specifically focusing upon Fishkin's educational (rather than only political) focus. As the work envisions equality of opportunity in *educational* rather than only *political* terms, the article also serves as an example of educational theorizing about traditionally political topics.[2]

This article shall first briefly explore Fishkin's analytical offerings, with a specific focus on the ways in which Fishkin advances a view on talent's conceptual coherence and applicability that counters a popular account of the same material's implicit relation to matters of educational opportunity. Following that critique, the article reconsiders talent by first investigating its conceptual coherence and then arguing for two legitimate uses of it as a criterion for some forms of equal access to certain educational opportunities. In this, the article compares *political* analyses with *educational* analyses of talent and educational opportunities. While respecting that distinction, the article concludes with a short statement of potential limitations to that view and the defense(s) of talent offered at the core of this article.

2. A partial overview of Fishkin's project

In recent work, Fishkin has helpfully enriched understandings of equality of opportunity as a feature of distributive justice schemes. In what follows, this article engages a small slice of Fishkin's larger project in order to make minimal claims about talent as a criterion for access to educational opportunities. Though the presentation of his arguments will be incomplete, that work shall be faithful to the relevant portions of his analyses as they address the central aims of the article.[3]

In essence, Fishkin's larger argument refocuses attention from the difficulties of ensuring that opportunities are appropriately equal (in either their quantitative distribution or qualitative value) towards a more nuanced understanding of the types of opportunities and opportunity structures that ought to be attractive under a wide range of distributive justice theories. In this, he presses for a more *developmental* focus in theorizing desirable opportunity structures.

Of course, in this, Fishkin engages influential accounts of equality of opportunity (with contributions by John Rawls (1971, 2001) and Ronald Dworkin (2000) each receiving considerable attention alongside formal egalitarian and luck egalitarian conceptions). In response to what he regards as shortcomings of these approaches to equality of opportunity (whether they be freestanding or embedded within theories of distributive justice), Fishkin supplants these accounts of equal opportunity with his theory of *opportunity pluralism*.

Opportunity pluralism suggests that a society is better organized when it resists endorsing opportunity structures leading to *bottlenecks,* defined here as circumstances in which individuals need to clear narrow or restrictive avenues of access in pursuit of greater opportunities or valuable lived experiences. In one of his recurring examples of a bottleneck, Fishkin imagines a society focused upon a big test, upon which one's successfully competitive performance in adolescence grants access to a wide range of desirable professions (Fishkin, 2014, p. 13). Though members of this big test society have varied life goals, they must all compete according to the metrics of the one big test. Competition within such a bottleneck is anathema to Fishkin's opportunity pluralism, in which, inter alia, a society's opportunity structures acknowledge many goals and paths towards achieving them.

Opportunity pluralism offers a number of interesting insights and normative principles, such that much meaningful secondary literature has been penned in its wake,[4] but its treatment of the specific issue of talent deserves focused attention.

Fishkin's contribution to theorizing equality of opportunity contains many intriguing portions and pieces, ripe for additional study and application. Perhaps chief among these is the way in which Fishkin addresses meritorious criteria for the just distribution of opportunities. For instance, popular egalitarian interpretations of Rawlsian fair equality of opportunity (moderated by the difference principle, and invoked under conditions of equality of basic liberties), one's life chances or opportunities may be contingent upon one's natural talent.[5] In many ways, it is to interpretations of this account of natural and social contingencies, especially focused upon talent, that Fishkin is responding.[6] As such, let us now closely attend to the concept of talent relative to Fishkin's opportunity pluralism, highlighting the ways in which it differs from that interpretation of Rawlsian treatment.[7]

2.1. Fishkin's response to an interpretation of Rawls on talent

Rawls' influential theory of justice, 'justice as fairness', significantly refers to the role that talent, as a specific *natural* contingency impacting the life chances available to persons, should play in the distribution of social and political opportunities.[8] According to a liberal equality interpretation of Rawls, social background ought have no bearing upon one's access to opportunities.[9] The idea here is that:

> '... [T]hose who are at the same level of talent and ability, and have the same willingness to use them, should have the same prospects of success regardless of their initial place in the social system ... ' (Rawls, A Theory of Justice, 1971, p. 73)

In sum, many egalitarian analyses of Rawls's work interpret his theory as attempting to control for social background while endorsing differences in opportunities that can be traced to disparities in natural talents between persons.[10] Arguably, according to this egalitarian interpretation of Rawls, the talented person evidences a measure of merit, indicative of the degree to which they deserve the advantages that flow form their use of talent. Moreover, under this egalitarian interpretation, justice requires that two persons of identical natural talent have identical opportunities. An injustice (on this issue) occurs if (and only if) differences in social background determine differences in opportunities. Talent serves as an acceptable and meritorious criterion for access to opportunities (Fishkin, 2014, p. 56).

Unsurprisingly, given Rawls' influence, rigorous academic works, public discourse, and policy conversations alike, seem to draw upon this egalitarian interpretation of the justified role that natural talent might play in allocating opportunities to persons, contrasting natural talent with the far more suspect influence of social factors (Fishkin, 2014, p. 87). These perspectives, including views from what Fishkin calls the 'casual popular science of genetics', suggest that opportunities might be justly distributed only if they are agnostic to one's social background while heavily beholden to the allotments and configuration of one's, purportedly natural, talent (ibid). This view, that a society can distinguish between natural and social characteristics and that, by so doing, it has identified a morally relevant criterion for apportioning opportunities amongst claimants, is presented as something of a foil for a portion of Fishkin's arguments regarding opportunity pluralism.

Fishkin suggests that natural contingencies, such as talent, do not deserve an elevated status relative to social contingencies. Fishkin holds that a society has no reason to treat one set of contingencies as morally significant in contrast to the other. Fishkin argues this by, *inter alia*, asserting that to speak of talents as though they are solely natural is misleading and ultimately conceptually incoherent. Fishkin writes that: '... talents result from a complex interaction between a person, with all of her potentialities, and various developmental opportunities that unlock and shape those potentialities into developed traits, abilities, and talents.' (Fishkin, 2014, p. 35, fn 38). In short, talent is neither natural nor social; it is necessarily the force of both inputs working in tandem.

Yet, even if natural contingencies could be disaggregated from the social variety (and he holds that they could not), Fishkin argues that this distinction leads, in many ways, to an unsuitable criterion for the distribution of opportunities. The logic of this distinction inclines a society to focus on how it might control for the 'wrong' type of contingency, preventing it from contaminating one's progression to a universally desired goal (Fishkin, 2014, p. 88). Said differently, building upon Fishkin's earlier concerns regarding the relative myopia of the big test society and its tendency to result in opportunity bottlenecks, treating a potential distinction between natural and social contingencies inclines a society to pose the wrong questions of justice relative to its opportunity structures. It presents an overly simplistic view of what the society might wish to avoid, rather than creating a context in which one might advance nuanced questions of what one might be or do through a society's opportunity structure. In this, Fishkin suggests posing *developmental* questions of equality of opportunity, moving away from the meritorious thinking that suggests that the difficult work of justice largely rests in circumventing morally arbitrary influences (namely, social rather than natural contingencies[11]).

To review, Fishkin finds fault in the popular conceptual orientation (arguably, though not definitively, partially owed to, or at least popularized by 'liberal equality' interpretations of Rawls) of a) distinguishing between natural and social contingencies and b) using that distinction to hold the view that controlling for the influence of one category of contingencies (i.e. social) largely maintains justice in a system aspiring to provide equal opportunity for those therein. Fishkin rejects these two inclinations finding that they can (and often do) lead to bottlenecks (of the big test variety) and are insufficiently explanatory of the complex factors that develop persons in any given configuration of potentialities.

As such, it is tempting to read Fishkin as having delivered a recent and fully devastating argument against talent as a criterion for access to opportunities within a just social system. Through Fishkin's work in response to interpretations of Rawls' theorizing on talent as a natural contingency rightfully granting access to opportunities, one might be led to think that talent is a conceptually incoherent and poor indicator of merit and thus always an inappropriate criterion for access to opportunities. In what follows, this article shall argue that this is an overstatement of Fishkin's offering (in fact, it ignores elements of his own claims), especially in regards to developmental opportunities. Though Fishkin does not offer this precise formulation, it may be helpful to employ a nuanced and quite essential distinction between regarding talent as 'a basic criterion fully determining access to opportunities' and talent as 'a guide towards the identification of developmentally useful opportunities'. In its focus on the possibility of the latter, the article avoids the aforementioned overstatement of Fishkin's conclusions on this matter by asking whether talent may indeed be a useful criterion (amongst many) in distributing specific resources on the basis of their developmental potential for specific persons. To make this claim, this article will more fully discuss these ideas within the context of explicitly educational resources, suggesting when, if ever, one may defend 'talent' as a criterion of access to these developmentally useful educational resources.[12]

3. Reviewing the analysis towards reconsidering talent

As made apparent in the preceding section, Fishkin's project widens the scope of analysis regarding equal opportunities. By focusing on bottlenecks as an essential problem to overcome on a path to greater justice, Fishkin re-contextualizes (what stand as) the relevant concepts in equal opportunity efforts. In this, Fishkin identifies the major types of bottlenecks.[13] For present purposes, this article will focus upon developmental bottlenecks as they contain the features most commonly underdiscussed in equal opportunity discourses.

Therefore, it might be right to state that this developmental focus is not limited to one section of Fishkin's project but is at the very center of his theory. Fishkin gives rather significant weight to the notion that equal opportunity is valuable because of its developmental implications (rather than, say, resting upon some deontological claim) (Fishkin, 2014, pp. 2–3, 41–48). This developmental focus inclines Fishkin to often speak about education (or more, precisely, largely about schooling and parenting) but I do not think he is quite thoughtful enough about how his theory is essentially educational because of its developmental focus (as more fully explored below). In any case, education serves as a quite useful example for a more developmental approach to opportunities.

Within that context, what follows will consider how this developmental focus allows for (and, arguably, requires) a meaningful appraisal of talent, potentially in the service of further distributive considerations. In pursuing some insights from Fishkin's work on talent within the developmental theory of opportunity pluralism, the article extends his arguments as educational, rather than only political, in nature, showcasing why talent serves as an important criterion for access to developmentally useful educational opportunities.[14]

Again, it should be noted that the following argument identifies talent as a useful indicator, determining a type of developmental efficacy. This need not entail a fully realized distributive scheme of educational resources. That application is beyond the scope of this article. Rather, as shall be argued below, this account of talent is presented as helpful in determining the underlying justifications that might inform the creation of such a distributive structure.

Fishkin and others offer good evidence that talent ought to be regarded with some (at least initial) suspicion when employed as a criterion for access to social advantage, with educational opportunities serving as one recurring example of this problem. However, these accounts of (and potential solutions to) the problem(s) of talent primarily address the political dimensions of the phenomenon in this context. That is, they point to the ways in which 'natural talent' ought not serve as a meritorious criterion for access to education opportunities as, at its base, talent seems an undeserved or morally irrelevant quality of persons (if it can be said to exist in a manner that can be usefully isolated so as to serve in this role) and, thereby, has no basis for complicating the default conclusions of a more explicitly egalitarian approach.

But, as shall be evidenced below, if one maintains a developmental focus, one might indeed pursue a limited defense of talent, understood in more fully educational terms, as justifiably useful in addressing some otherwise frustrating bottleneck problems.

As mentioned above, Fishkin holds that multiple types of bottlenecks exist and require slightly different responses so as to realize the aims of opportunity pluralism. In this context, one might defend talent as a non-arbitrary criterion for access to some developmentally useful opportunities. Fishkin's identifies developmental bottlenecks as those circumstances in which persons are constrained in accessing further developmental opportunities (Fishkin, 2014, pp. 156, 173). Having identified this specific type of bottleneck, observe that the irrelevance of a particular criterion encountered under one analytic perspective or category of problem does not entail its irrelevance across all others. For example, while height is an irrelevant criterion for one's eligibility to run for public office, it may serve as a fine (and, perhaps, necessary) criterion for access to an amusement park attraction or broader concerns under the category of physical safety relative to specific equipment; the criterion of height is non-arbitrary in the second instances. As such, perhaps recent work on the moral relevance of talent deserves additional attention as talent might be salient only to certain types of developmental bottlenecks or certain analyses of bottlenecks more broadly.

To be clear, when viewed within a political analysis, talent can indeed be cast as a morally irrelevant criterion resulting in bottlenecks that perpetuate unjust outcomes. As such, societies ought to remain vigilant against the ways in which criteria of talent can visit unjust political outcomes upon their members when applied to a wide variety of *political* opportunities.[15] Nonetheless, talent may be defended as an appropriate criterion for some *educational* opportunities. Indeed, this view is consistent with Fishkin's own view, which can be fruitfully extended even as we are careful to limit its reach in specific ways.

3.1. The existence of talent

Towards furthering Fishkin's contributions by providing a limited defense of talent as a morally relevant criterion for access to some educational opportunities, the article aims to interrogate the possibility of a coherent conceptualization of talent. Following this, the political value of attention to talent in distributive contexts shall be suggested. Finally, this value will be contrasted with the educational value of attention to talent, arguing that it affords talent a non-arbitrary relevance consistent with the central developmental aims of Fishkin's theory of opportunity pluralism. As this relevance is not absolute, the article shall also suggest (though not explore in depth) some limits to the use of talent as such a criterion, with particular focus on systematic limitations.

3.2. Is the concept of talent coherent?

Though Fishkin offers a strong critique of natural talent as an appropriate criterion for (among other types) educational opportunities, these arguments leave open the possibility for exploration of the concept of talent itself. Recall, a portion of his critique hinges upon the incomprehensibility of natural talent as conceptually disentangled from the influence of social contingencies, but Fishkin does not suggest that talent itself is a wholly incomprehensible concept. He convincingly argues that the concept of *natural* talent, as a discreet contingency unto itself, is unsatisfying. This does not mean that the concept of talent itself cannot be coherently conceptualized.

Though this may seem a minor point, it is nonetheless important to acknowledge that the concept of talent is not wholly incoherent – as might appear to be the case via Fishkin's critique of natural talent.[16] Despite worries about the degree to which an appeal to natural talent actually supports further advantaging persons on the basis of social contingencies, there seems to be no immediate tension internal to general usage of the concept itself, such that talent cannot be meaningfully discussed as a characteristic of persons linked to their possible performance, without the special normative weight (i.e. desert of additional opportunity advantage) expected by the egalitarian arguments to which Fishkin is responding.

Let us consider the following example:

Ms. Sterling, a teacher at the local school, receives a request from the leaders of a prestigious summer program to recommend 'musically talented students'. Having heard a new student in the school, Isiah, masterfully play the piano, she had previously described him to others as musically talented. Upon learning that Isiah has undergone an intense regimen of piano lessons and a strict schedule of practice before moving to the district, Ms. Sterling might proceed in a number of ways, two of which follow:

a. Ms. Sterling may be less inclined to describe Isiah as 'talented'. Though evidence of Isiah's musical mastery is equivalent in moments before and after Ms. Sterling is made aware of the inputs and experiences that have informed his performance, she may think that the source of mastery matters and that some sources are talent-eligible, while others are not. Ms. Smith may well assert that, since she has evidence that supports the fact that Isiah's performance is, at least partially, the result of instruction and not purely the manifestation of some inborn measure of mastery, it cannot be called 'talent' and she cannot recommend him for the valuable opportunity.

b. Ms. Sterling might continue to refer to Isiah as talented. To her mind, the source(s) of the performance matters little for the legitimate use of the label of 'talented'. She is happy to recommend him for the valuable summer opportunity.

If it is true (which seems likely) that most persons who employ the concept of talent (in contexts similar to this example), do so in ways that more closely mirror the second possibility rather than the first (i.e. they do not need to investigate the sources of apparent talent in order to refer to a performance as sufficient evidence of talent), it would seem that general usage of the concept of talent does little more than identify the capacity for some performance.[17] The existence of that capacity may or may not represent any desert or need relative to further opportunities; it stands only as an indicator of one's potential to perform.

This understanding of talent is far less troubling than the notion that Fishkin pushes against (i.e. natural talent as understood by the Rawlsian egalitarian), and yet it may allow us to maintain the fine conclusions of Fishkin's opportunity pluralism.

3.3. The value of talent

Having established that talent might serve as a non-normative characteristic of persons, we can push slightly further to now ask whether talent can, in some cases or contexts, be understood as valuable such that it carries normative weight in the allocation of opportunities. What follows shall consider two contexts for this analysis, the political and the pedagogical.[18]

3.3.1. Political

Without fully revisiting them here, note that Fishkin's arguments suggest why one would do well to be suspicious of the political or social dimensions of employing talent in considerations of who ought to receive specific goods. Though focused on natural talents, his argument regarding the suitability of talent as a criterion for political/social advantage is similarly (though not identically) effective against a more general view of talent. As a political standard, a focus on talent as an indicator of desert may incline a system towards greater uniformity of the sort that his opportunity pluralism wishes to avoid.

That stated, an assessment of talent employed in the service of distributing opportunities could be legitimately useful in a political context. For example, if a society has good reason to determine (at least) a rough appraisal of candidates' suitability for holding public office and performing the required tasks thereof, a democratic, public, and appropriately legible appraisal of talent (as a statement of the degree of suitability given likely performance in the role) would be defensible. Talent, broadly understood, may indeed be useful in determining eligibility for holding valued and/or important social positions, even as that usefulness conflicts with other political aims.[19]

Beyond evaluating meritorious desert (i.e. that good opportunities are reserved for those good enough to deserve them), a society might use talent to determine which of its members are most in need of specific goods that they can convert into valuable outcomes. While this may realize political ends, this usage of talent as a criterion for accessing opportunities can certainly be explored as developmental (*a la* Fishkin), and thus educational, at its core.

3.3.2. Pedagogical

A more developmental focus can be contrasted with the political analysis described above. Rather than concern itself with the political logic and attentions of how best to distribute valued yet scarce goods amongst persons, this focus is essentially pedagogical as it attends to what persons might become and how those potentials might best be realized. To be clear, this mode of analysis is not wholly detached or separated from political concerns (nb: it is likely that in some moments, political questions must be answered in order to attend to pedagogical aims). Rather, this analytical context finds salience in issues likely unexplored or under-explored through a political analysis.

Without compromising the aims of an opportunity pluralistic society, this developmental analysis can embrace some non-arbitrary uses of talent as a salient criterion in the distribution of opportunities including, and exceeding, those traditionally attached to education (i.e. schooling, parenting, etc.). Below, two examples are offered.

3.3.3. Using talent to navigate the non-fungibility of educational opportunities

In some cases, developmental opportunities visit remarkably different outcomes upon those who possess and make use of them. Rather than a unified or universal value (as might be more common for political opportunities), these educational opportunities are valuable in their specific and unique effect(s) upon a person and access to them is not a matter of merit but of use-value. For example, a person with talent X might be able, on the basis of that talent, to make use of developmental opportunity Y towards some valued outcome Z. If the same developmental opportunity Y were instead given to a person who does not possess the talent necessary to convert that opportunity to outcome Z, the educational opportunity would (in reference to outcome Z) have been lost.[20] With a developmental focus, an analysis of educational opportunity is more sharply attuned to the fact that a system of opportunity distribution is not merely shuffling fungible opportunities between persons. A poorly considered distribution may result in lost developmental opportunities for specific persons as well as the aggregate group of persons amongst whom limited resources might be distributed; as such, an appraisal of talent, in the service of its use as a criterion for identification of and access to developmentally useful educational opportunities, is non-arbitrary and indeed valuable.

Fishkin explores a similar set of ideas in describing 'developmental bottlenecks' (though he uses the term *capacities* rather than *talents* [potentially, to avoid confusion with natural talents] in this analysis, the underlying concept is identical) (Fishkin, 2014, pp. 156–158). In short, some developmental opportunities or resources exist such that one may not make use of them given that person's previous developmental achievements or talents. This is important information for an educator (broadly construed as a teacher or designer of developmental opportunity systems) who must make informed decisions about how to contribute to learners' good development.

3.3.4. Using talent to assess education need

As previously introduced, a developmentally-focused analysis of talent within opportunity structures could identify developmental need in a pedagogically valuable way. Following Fishkin's identification of developmental bottlenecks, a distributive system could tailor its opportunity distribution to prioritize providing educational opportunities to those who exhibit a *lack* of the specific talent(s) necessary to make use of some valued opportunities. For example, in this potential distributive system, if it were the case that a student, Elaine, currently lacks the literacy talent necessary for further study of, say, distant cultures and geographic regions, a talent-sensitive system of opportunity distribution keyed towards her developmental benefit would have interest in identifying her as a student in need of literacy-developing opportunities and thereby providing the real opportunities of which she has need.[21] In such cases, a less talent-sensitive evaluation risks missing the developmental usefulness of these opportunities and might thereby less deftly locate and address Elaine's need; as such, an assessment of talent, as an important evaluative criterion in prioritizing access allocations according to the determinant of benefit via specifically needed educational opportunities, is non-arbitrary and, indeed, quite useful.[22]

According to Fishkin (2014, p. 132), an opportunity pluralistic society ought to adhere to an *anti-bottleneck principle* such that it expands and maintains an array of both formal and informal developmental opportunities. For the reasons presented above, this expansion effort is well-served by assessments that rely upon the identification of talent. Sensitivity to talent can helpfully organize and prioritize the potential permutations of matches between persons and educational opportunities, effectively realizing much of the expansion such a society would seek. Fishkin's (2014, p. 56) arguments against natural talent identify shortcomings of natural talent's use as a meritorious criterion for access to opportunity. Though Fishkin does not explicitly build from that critique to identify 'talent' as indicative of something other than one's merit, reframing talent in this way secures much of the aims of Fishkin's theory of opportunity pluralism.

Under the two examples provided above, talent serves as a non-arbitrary criterion for identification of and access to developmentally useful educational opportunities. While Fishkin's caution against (natural) talent serving as a criterion for access to opportunities (educational or otherwise) is compelling when analyzed from a political perspective, a switch in conceptual frames, towards the very pedagogically-oriented developmental focus at the core of Fishkin's project, provides good reason to support talent as a criterion for determining developmentally useful opportunities that are, in essence, educational. Indeed, depending upon the aims of a given distributive project (which might be influenced by the developmental focus articulated above), this account of talent may prove useful in the structuring of specific systems of educational access.

4. Developmental and political: some limitations

Though Fishkin invokes traditional educational examples (schools, universities, etc.) for his work on opportunity pluralism, his work does not seem to embrace his developmental focus towards the way in which the conceptualization itself is educational. As such, it misses the opportunity to identify its justification of expanded opportunity structures as an expression of essentially educational analyses of what are largely understood as social and political phenomena (e.g. the fair/appropriate distribution of opportunities or resources) (Frankel, 1971).

An extension of Fishkin's developmental focus might allow his theory to rest within a larger educational, rather than only political, approach to justice (Thompson, 2016). From this analytical perspective, talent can be used as a criterion for access to educational opportunities in formally educational contexts, but it might also be employed in the service of the broader developmental aims within a society. Here, one might envision Fishkin's opportunity pluralism pushing for the organization of civil society such that a diversity of values and recognition of the unique existing and desired talents of persons is foregrounded.[23] Without finely detailing what such attentions might create, it may be wise to instead briefly focus on the limitations to such a system of talent appraisal in the organization and distribution of educational opportunities.

First, educational analyses of attention to talent-sensitive opportunity structures will occur alongside political analyses of the same. Though a use of talent as an educational criterion for access to the types of educational opportunities earlier described might not, in one instance, run afoul of the standards of justice in that analytical frame, it might very well do so in another (i.e. the traditional political analysis). Stated differently, a system of (educational) opportunity allocation needs to be sensitive to the pedagogical *as well as* (rather than *instead of*) the political. Care should be taken to ensure that the pursuit of educationally desirable circumstances do not create extremely undesirable political situations. Again, without providing necessarily detailed examples, one can readily envision that in a world marked by the impacts of racism, sexism, classism, ableism and more the analytical view of the usefulness of talent founded upon the expansion of Fishkin's developmentally-focused opportunity pluralism, may need to be limited (or otherwise complemented) in cases which run afoul of a political analysis of justice[24]

Second, and more specifically, care must be taken to ensure that the use of talent as a criterion for access to educational opportunities does not result in situations of systemic or aggregate advantage, particularly in ways that correlate to the existing patterns of power referenced above. Talent bottlenecks are seemingly unavoidable; the work of education is found in addressing them as they occur anew in persons developing within a complex world. Though talent bottlenecks will occur (for example, in a student who must possess some talent for X before she can begin to learn Y), a focus upon addressing them as developmentally undesirable should do much to resist the appraisal of persons within such bottlenecks as 'undesirables'.[25] Even so, the evaluative dimension of the criterion of talent might lead to systematized stigma or subordinate status. While these undesirable outcomes are usually well understood via a political analysis, they have a real developmental dimension (Steele & Aronson, 1995), such that efforts against them can be justified by the educational focus of opportunity pluralism.

Third, the use of talent as a criterion for access to developmentally useful educational opportunities ought not encourage competition between students/claimants. To the extent that talent has been justified within this article as a criterion for access of the sort described in the previous sections, that justification has been embedded within an expanded version of Fishkin's opportunity pluralism. That framework holds that the avoidable bottlenecks that occur from competitive systems threaten the abiding aims of the distributive project. As such, talent's use as a criterion should be limited insofar as doing so prevents bottleneck-creating systems of competition for educational opportunities.

Finally, the arguments provided in the preceding pages rest within broader aims of equal opportunity. As such, these arguments for the defensibility of talent as a criterion for access to educational resources would surely need to be reconsidered for contexts loyal to some other primary determinant of access to opportunities (i.e. rather than equality) or indifferent to the developmental usefulness of opportunities. As these are well beyond the scope of the current claim and its arguments, these limitations are acknowledged but not engaged.

5. Conclusions

In what has been presented, the article has accomplished its core aim of establishing within Fishkin's commitments to opportunity pluralism, a limited defense of talent as a criterion for access to developmentally useful educational opportunities.

Having agreed with Fishkin's analysis of natural talent, the article has offered a view of talent as capacity to perform, such that the conceptual coherence of talent has been established and its use in/as pedagogical assessment (shown valuable in the service of broader distributive aims) defended. This developmental focus has been contrasted with a political analysis, such that Fishkin's opportunity pluralism's suitability as an educational theory of social/political phenomena has been suggested. In outlining some parameter limitations for this approach to talent, this article has pointed to the ways in which the educational and political analyses might influences one another and a society's appraisal of each.

In sum, this article has not attempted to offer a radical new conclusion regarding talent in educational contexts. Indeed, talent is already often invoked in educational spaces. Instead, this work has focused on one large project (i.e. Fishkin's opportunity pluralism) in order to provide a more detailed consideration of a specific concern, namely, why we ought not to let our worries about talent fully remove all accounts of it from our view of the just distribution of educational opportunities. To do so, mistakes the educational for the political and obliges the former to only the standards of the latter. In light of that, we might have good reason to revisit and review other status quo conclusions in the field of education. If we can find new categories for arguments supporting talent as a criterion for access to educational opportunities, perhaps we might do the same for other portions of our educational world.

Notes

1. My analysis of talent is concerned with its potentially defensible role as a feature within a broad project of distribution loyal to equal opportunity goals. That is, I do not aim to show that talent itself serves as a primary determinant for access to educational opportunity, but rather that is a defensible evaluative criterion of whether an important determinant (developmentally useful opportunity) is achievable.
2. See, (Thompson, 2016).
3. With regrets, given constraints of space and subject, this article cannot provide a fuller exploration of Fishkin's contribution to scholarship on equality of opportunity or provide a detailed statement of how this contribution is situated in relation to other competing approaches and foci. Readers interested in this additional context would do well to see, (Fishkin, 2016) (Wisnewski, 2016).
4. E.g., see The Brookings Institution (2014).
5. More specifically, one's life chances are a function of one's talents [and willingness to use them] amid a structure of opportunities. And, of course, Rawls' theory takes one's natural talent *and effort* to be at issue. For a number of reasons, I would like to bracket effort, holding it as a constant in/across all cases in which talent is discussed, analyzed, or compared in the remainder of this paper.
6. Though Fishkin is also, to a large degree, responding to Dworkin, I will focus my present attentions only on a subset of issues relevant to his Rawlsian critique.
7. It should be observed that the question of whether this interpretation accurately captures Rawls' nuance is somewhat beside the point. What matters is that the interpretation has gained power in the wake of the theory.

   Rawls himself pressed against this interpretation by indicating that his Difference Principle sought to ameliorate undeserved differences in natural and social advantage, but the interpretation (i.e., the liberal equality interpretation) is invoked by lay and initiated audiences. For example, see (Ryan, 2011) and (Lazenby, 2016).
8. Though various terms as used, ('endowments', 'assets', 'abilities', etc) in Rawls's writing and the secondary literature, I refer to 'talents' as a general term for concepts within this category. See, (Rawls, A Theory of Justice, 1971) and (Rawls, Justice as fairness : a restatement, 2001)
9. Of course, very much might be said about the examples that Rawls invokes (and omits in his efforts) to make clear his distinction between natural and social characteristics. See, for example (Mills, 2009).
10. Rawls himself is quite insistent that this is not the case, but many have pointed to the ways in which his theory seemingly trades on the distinction between social and natural contingencies (despite his claims to move beyond them). See, (Pogge, 1989, pp. 164 & 166) and (Daniels, 1985).
11. In this, Fishkin's work edges close to the Capabilities Approach. Though he does not engage this connection fully, foundational works in that body of literature raise similar and related questions (especially as related to education). See, (Nussbaum, 2011; Saito, 2003; Sen & Nussbaum, 1993).
12. In what follows, I do not detail how particular types of educational opportunities (K-12, postsecondary, formal, informal, etc.) might complicate this analysis. Such distinctions, while useful in many ways, are outside of the focus of this work. That said, I wish to suggest an encompassing view of developmentally useful educational opportunities, inclusive of these and many other subtypes.
13. Including 'qualification bottlenecks', 'developmental bottlenecks', and 'instrumental good bottlenecks', (Fishkin, 2014, pp. 156–158).
14. In this, I draw upon Charles Frankel's (1971) distinction between the 'meritocratic' and 'educational' conceptions of equality of opportunity. Briefly invoked by Fishkin (2014, p. 80), Frankel's argument lays the foundation for the developmental focus of Fishkin's theorizing, suggesting that an educational focus yields conclusions quite different from that of a meritocratic (which can be closely linked to political theory) analysis.
15. This includes the political analysis of educational opportunities.
16. In some ways, Fishkin sidesteps this by, in a number of instances, writing about capacities of persons rather than talents. Though that term is certainly not novel within this tradition of analysis, Fishkin's use leans away from talent, as identified in this article. Still, I follow his use of language below to further link to Fishkin's project.
17. Unless otherwise noted, 'talent' will be used in this way (rather than in reference to the concept of 'natural talent') for the remainder of this article.
18. In what follows I will interchangeably use the terms *pedagogical, educational*, and *developmental.*

19. Though a comparison of talent's political usefulness in particular instances juxtaposed against its role in systemic patterns of opportunity structures within a given society is meaningful and likely deserves much additional attention, it shall not be explored further here. The focus of this paper prevents a full engagement with those issues and can highlight their importance only in the service of further establishing that a society's system of opportunity allocation can be quite morally complex (i.e., endorsing divergent conclusions) when invoking the salience of talent.
20. Again, this point seems to be compatible with Fishkin's own comments on developmental opportunities (2014, pp. 124–128), and Martha Nussbaum's (2011) version of the capabilities approach. This point marks talent's use as a salient determinant of developmental usefulness (including, inter alia, some evaluation of 'efficacy').
21. I am grateful to an anonymous reviewer who flags that an educator ought to be aware of both *extant* and *potential* talents.
22. I must clarify that this example certainly lends support to the notion that talent is a relevant guide to the nature or character of resources that persons ought to enjoy. To some readers, this might seem too minor a role to influence distribution. But, in a world without only fully fungible educational resources, such guidance is rather likely to influence the distribution of specific resources. It is unlikely that persons will have identical or even 'nonidentical-yet-equal-in-cumulative-number-and-degree' collections of socially recognized talents. As such, talent's guidance regarding the types of resources persons ought to enjoy will very likely prompt complex distributive considerations (including those about *amounts* of resources) across these meaningful differences between persons. I thank an anonymous reviewer for pointing me towards this subtle issue.
23. This strongly realizes Fishkin's (2014, pp. 131–132) principles of opportunity pluralism.
24. Interestingly, as evidenced in the substance of this article, the reverse might also be true. Policies resulting from a political analysis of talent may need to be attenuated if they run afoul of the educational aims of a developmental analysis.
25. Regrettably, one need only look towards perceptions of students within remedial educational programs to see evidence of the existence of such disappointing attitudes. See also, (Nora & Garcia, 2001) (Lesley, 2004).

Disclosure statement

No potential conflict of interest was reported by the author(s).

ORCID

Winston C. Thompson http://orcid.org/0000-0001-6474-0778

References

Bailey, R. (2007). Talent development and the luck problem. *Sport, Ethics and Philosophy (Official Journal of the British Philosophy of Sport Association)*, *1*(3), 367–377. https://doi.org/10.1080/17511320701676999

Beckwith, F. J. (1999). The "No One Deserves His or Her Talents" argument for affirmative action: A critical analysis. *Social Theory and Practice*, *25*(1), 53–60. https://doi.org/10.5840/soctheorpract19992512

Daniels, N. (1985). *Just health care*. Cambridge University Press.

Dworkin, R. (2000). *Sovereign Virtue the theory and practice of equality*. Harvard University Press.

Elford, G. (2016). Social class, merit and equality of opportunity in education. *Res Publica*, *22*(3), 267–284. https://doi.org/10.1007/s11158-015-9280-3

Fishkin, J. (2014). *Bottlenecks: A new theory of equality of opportunity*. Oxford University Press.

Fishkin, J. (2016). Bottlenecks, disability, and preference-formation: A reply. *Social Philosophy Today*, *32*, 189–197. https://doi.org/10.5840/socphiltoday201671529

Frankel, C. (1971). Equality of opportunity. *Ethics*, *81*(3), 191–211. https://doi.org/10.1086/291810

Kotzee, B., & Martin, C. (2013). Who should go to university? Justice in university admissions. *Journal of Philosophy of Education*, *47*(4), 623–641. https://doi.org/10.1111/1467-9752.12044

Lazenby, H. (2016). What is equality of opportunity in education? *Theory and Research in Education*, *14*(1), 65–76. https://doi.org/10.1177/1477878515619788

Lesley, M. (2004). Refugees from reading: Students' perceptions of "Remedial" literacy pedagogy. *Reading Research and Instruction*, *44*(1), 62–86. https://doi.org/10.1080/19388070409558421

Merisotis, J. (2015). *America needs talent: Attracting, educating & deploying the 21st-century workforce*. RosettaBooks.

Mills, C. (2009). Rawls on race/race in Rawls. *The Southern Journal of Philosophy*, *47*(S1), 161–184. https://doi.org/10.1111/j.2041-6962.2009.tb00147.x

Nora, A., & Garcia, V. (2001). The role of perceptions of remediation on the persistence of developmental students in higher education. Paper presented at the annual meeting of the Association for the Study of Higher Education.

Nussbaum, M. (2011). *Creating capabilities*. Harvard University Press.

Petrović, N. (2009). Equality of opportunity and personal identity. *Acta Analytica*, *24*(2), 97–111. https://doi.org/10.1007/s12136-009-0046-4

Pogge, T. W. (1989). *Realizing rawls*. Cornell University Press.

Rawls, J. (1971). *A theory of justice*. Harvard University Press.

Rawls, J. (2001). *Justice as fairness: A restatement*. Harvard University Press.

Ryan, P. (2011, November 15). Saving the American idea: Rejecting fear, envy, and the politics of divisionThe Heritage Foundation. https://www.heritage.org/political-process/report/saving-the-american-idea-rejecting-fear-envy-and-the-politics-division

Saito, M. (2003). Amartya sen's capability approach to education: A critical exploration. *Journal of Philosophy of Education*, *37*(1), 17–33. https://doi.org/10.1111/1467-9752.3701002

Sen, A., & Nussbaum, M. (1993). *The quality of life*. Clarendon Press.

Slote, M. (2013). *Education and human values: Reconciling talent with and ethics of care*. Routledge.

Steele, C. M., & Aronson, J. (1995). Stereotype threat and the intellectual test performance of African Americans. *Journal of Personality and Social Psychology*, *69*(5), 797–811. https://doi.org/10.1037/0022-3514.69.5.797

The Brookings Institution. (2014, April-May). *Bottlenecks: A new theory of equal opportunity*. https://www.brookings.edu/series/bottlenecks-a-new-theory-of-equal-opportunity/

Thompson, W. C. (2016). Rethinking discussions of justice in educational research: Formative justice, educational liberalism, and beyond. *Teachers College Record*, *118*(10), 1–16.

Vopat, M. C. (2011). Magnet schools, innate talent, and social justice. *Theory and Research in Education*, *9*(1), 59–72. https://doi.org/10.1177/1477878510394811

Wisnewski, J. J. (2016). Symposium on Joseph Fishkin's 'Bottlenecks'. *Review Journal of Political Philosophy*, *12*, 1–46.

Wolff, T. B., & Wolff, R. P. (2005). The pimple on Adonis's Nose: A dialogue on the concept of Merit in the affirmative action debate. *Hastings Law Journal*, *56*, 379.

China's making and governing of educational subjects as 'talent': A dialogue with Michel Foucault

Weili Zhao

ABSTRACT

As an imprint of Confucian culture, China's education intersects state governance in making and governing educational subjects as 'talent', an official translation of the Chinese term 'rencai' (literally, human-talent). Whereas the English word 'talent' itself denotes '[people with] natural aptitude or skill', 'talent' is currently mobilized in China not only as a globalized discourse that speaks to the most aspired educational subjects for the 21st century but also as a re-invoked cultural notion that relates to Confucian wisdom. Drawing upon Foucault's biopower hypothesis and Confucian thought, this paper leverages upon China's unique manipulation of 'talent' as certain skills and human subjects, both cultivable through education, to problematize China's talent making and governing in two dimensions. First, it unpacks the various technologies of power entangled in China's talent making and governing within its 'state governance' paradigm. Second, it unpacks Confucian thought as an archaeological prototype for China's present talent appeal, meanwhile explicating their divergences in defining 'human', 'talent', and the human-talent interpellation. In so doing, this paper makes two arguments. First, the linguistic notion of 'talent' functions as a Foucauldian apparatus of biopower, making (up) new kinds of people and normalizing a certain population as the objective/object of China's state governance. Second, CPC's re-invocation of Confucian talent discourses is more of a rhetorical strategy than an authentic cultural renaissance gesture.

Introduction

Education is primarily about making and governing types of human subjects (Popkewitz, 2007) as human capital, and the vision and mission of every nation-state are different. At the juncture of state governance and education, China is now mobilizing an explosive discourse of 'talent' (not 'human capital') as the official gloss of the Chinese term 'rencai' (literally, human-talent), designating both skills and a population of educational subjects cultivable and desirable in the 21st century. (To differentiate the multiple senses of 'talent' utilized in the Chinese context from its original English denotation of '[people with] natural aptitude/skill', linguistically I employ 'talent' to signify people with talent-skills, 'scholar-talent' for scholars labelled as talent, and 'talent-skills' and 'talent-people' to differentiate the different registers of talent.) For example, President Xi (2013, 2016, 2018) has sonorously called to 'convene talent from the world for [China's] use', treating talent as a valuable human resource crucial in enhancing China's global competitiveness. Accordingly, an educational–political–social-cultural *talent war* has erupted in full swing among provinces, regions, and universities, all striving to grab talent, domestic or overseas, through varied schemes (Roxburgh, 2017; China's official talent website http://rencai.people.com.cn/). Its escalated talent War 2.0 (Wang & Miao, 2018) is reconfiguring China's demographic and social structure at an unparalleled pace and scale.

China's stake of talent development at the juncture of education and state governance in enhancing its global competitiveness is first embodied in its state policies. The Hu Jintao administration (2003–2013) stipulates 'empowering China with talent' as its national development strategy (*rencai qiangguo zhanlue*) (Communist Party of China Central Committee and State Council 2003, hereafter CPC). China's 2010–2020 education plan is to 'make billions of high-quality laborers, millions of talent in various areas, and a large cohort of top-notched innovation talent' (The Medium-and-Long Term Educational Plan). China has since been forcefully tapping talent resources to 'build a large-scaled, well-structured, and high-quality talent cohort', aiming to turn China from a 'largely-populated nation to a largely talent-populated nation' (CPC, 2003). As its latest gesture, the Xi Jinping administration called to construct a globally competitive talent mechanism, i.e., an 'open, scientifically regulated, and efficiently operating *talent making and governing system*' (CPC, 2016).

This discourse of a 'talent making and governing system' (*rencai fazhan zhili tixi*) needs to be understood against the backdrop of China's 'state governance' (*guojia zhili*) paradigm stipulated in its 18th *People's Congress Report* (2012). There, it says, deepening China's reform all-round entails 'further modernizing its *state governance system and capacity*'. Please note 'governance system/capacity' are not my terms, although I will argue below they resonate well with Foucault's governmentality thinking. Rather, China has deliberately chosen 'state governance' from the modern politics and public administration field to replace the old and only one-word-different term of 'state government' (*guojia guanli*) (Feng, 2014). 'State governance' represents the first, fundamental, and revolutionary transformation in China's state governing structure and power redistribution (Heath, 2016; Stromseth et al., 2017). It redefines the single-ruling CPC from an authoritarian 'revolutionary party' (*geming dang*), as enacted in the Mao-Deng-Jiang administrations with total control over China's political, social, and economic issues, to a leading 'governing party' (*zhizheng dang*) after the 2002 Hu administration (Heath, 2016). That is, the CPC is anticipated to function as a 'stable, competent, rational bureaucratic actor capable of effectively governing its people' (ibid., 4), empowering China as a more democratic society.

It is true that commodifying knowledge in the neoliberal era has inevitably staked (higher) education as a competitive resource, thrusting all nation-states into a global auction for the high-skilled educational talent (Li & Lowe, 2016). China is no exception. Nevertheless, I argue that China's strategic appeal to 'talent' (not 'human capital') and China's talent making and governing at the juncture of education and state governance are more an imprint of Confucian educational culture than a mere effect of neoliberalization of education. For example, President Xi repeatedly re-invokes Confucian texts to clarify his viewpoints of the desirable talent in current China. Thus, rather than problematize the (in)effectiveness of China's new governance paradigm per se (Gong et al., 2017; Stromseth et al., 2017), this paper unpacks China's talent making and governing at the intersection of education and state governance in two dimensions. First, it borrows Foucault's biopower hypothesis to explicate the mechanisms-technologies entailed in classifying, selecting, and regulating talent as an object-objective at the interstices of sovereign power and biopower. Second, it historicizes China's talent appeal to its Confucian prototype to explicate possible transformations in defining 'human', 'talent', and their interpellation.

Drawing upon Foucault's biopower hypothesis helps render intelligible to the English world China's talent-governmentality in a neoliberal disciplinary-surveillance society, whereas historicizing the Confucian thought brings out its cultural uniqueness. Please note the word 'historicizing' is used here in a Foucauldian archaeological sense different from the common-sensical historicist way of tracking the linear development of certain ideas. That is, I do not track when the idea of talent first appears and its historical change. Rather, I unpack Confucian talent text as one archaeological prototype for today's talent appeal and juxtapose them for comparison. Together, this paper clarifies why 'talent', not 'human capital', is a preferred discourse for China to describe educational subjects and how the CPC re-invokes Confucian discourses in justifying its 21st-century state governing through education.

Foucault's biopower as a new form of governance

Foucault (2007, p. 1) conceptualizes 'biopower' as a 'set of mechanisms through which the basic biological features of the human species become the object of a political strategy, of a general strategy of power'. It embodies a turning point in his investigations from the history of disciplines to the art of governing and technologies of self, compelling Foucault to return to the question of subjectivity (Genel, 2006). Placing its stakes on life and population, 'biopower' re-conceptualizes power no longer as a unified juridical form but as a form of governmentality, that is, conduct of conduct among varying governing institutions and persons ordered through technologies of power. It relates to the change of human mentality to responding to the governance in modern society. Furthermore, it is bound up with and yet remains distinct from the old sovereign power to the extent that power can be discerned at the interstices where it had otherwise remained undetected (ibid.).

To Foucault, biopower emerged in the 17th-century Western society as a form of disciplinary power working on individual bodies, and in the second half of the 18th century as a normalizing power, targeted towards a certain population through regulating-administering their biological processes. While some scholars believe Foucault differentiates biopower as a 'disciplinary anatamopolitics of the body' (Hope, 2016, p. 887) from biopolitics of the population as focused on 'the species body … birth, morbidity, mortality, longevity' (Rabinow & Rose, 2006, p. 196), others uphold that Foucault uses biopower and biopolitics interchangeably (Hope, 2016; Mills, 2013). To Foucault (1978), biopower has enabled modern nation-states to foster 'numerous and diverse techniques for achieving the subjugations of bodies and the control of populations' (140). For example, in the 18th century, the 'private' and 'public' medical practices were reassembled and transposed into a considered form of 'noso-politics' (Foucault, 1984) which engages health and sickness not only as being personal and social but also as a scientific and political issue to be regulated through security mechanism.

According to Foucault, noso-politics defines the nature of, and the interpellation among, health/sickness, life/population (the biological body), and power (technologies of power) with three features. First, the state is no longer the centre of initiative, organization, and control. Rather than an effect of a vertical state intervention, noso-politics as a problem of health and sickness emerges at a multitude of sites and social instances. Second, health and sickness become the new function through which power is exercised across society through apparatuses and technologies of medical service, economic regulation, and general rules of hygiene. Simply put, noso-politics 'inscribes the specific question of the sickness of the poor within the general problem of the health of populations' (278). Third, the biological 'body' of individuals and populations is no longer merely the indicator of health and sickness. Instead, it becomes a symbol which attaches itself to various new variables such that some bodies become more utilizable, trainable, or more likely to survive than others. Thus, a technology of population forms to classify people according to their biological body conditions, and finer and more adequate power apparatuses appear to order population not merely as a problem but as 'an object of surveillance, analysis, intervention, modification' (ibid.).

Foucault's biopower as both discipline and biopolitics has been employed to examine different powers of technology in disciplinary, surveillance, and control society within and without schools. For example, scholars (Bryce et al., 2010; Hope, 2005, 2009; Kuehn, 2008; Taylor, 2014) have unpacked the complex interplay between elements of biopower, school monitoring devices like Internet software, cameras, biometrical devices and databases, and the student body. These research projects mostly corroborate Foucault's (1977) argument that discipline and surveillance devices, in making and normalizing the 'self-policing of the body', induce 'a state of conscious and permanent visibility that assures the automatic functioning of power' (201). Hope (2016) further argues that school monitoring devices not only objectify the student body through both disciplinary means and regulatory biopolitical management but also become sites for students to implode surveillance to souveillance as a subjectivity-performing medium. Outside of school, the Zhao (2017a) historicizes observation as China's civic education pedagogy in a way akin to yet not reducible to Foucault's panoptic gaze in the Western disciplinary societies. This paper examines the intersection between China's education and state governance, a characteristic unique to Confucian educational culture and yet rarely scrutinized so far.

Foucault's biopower hypothesis re-articulates power as partly moving away from the old sovereignty mechanism to a power relation of conduct among humans/institutions. This shift speaks to the intended structure of China's newly adopted 'state governance' paradigm and its talent making-governing dynamics. Specifically, China's current 'state governance' claims to redefine CPC no longer as an authoritarian 'revolutionary party' but as a leading 'governing party', a 'stable, competent, rational bureaucratic actor capable of effectively governing its people' (Heath, 2016, p. 4) toward building China into a more democratic society. Although the CPC still maintains itself in praxis as an authoritarian sovereign power (as my below analysis is to show), Foucault's biopower provides a theoretical lens for me to explore talent not as a given category, but as an apparatus through which power is localized and exercised through multiple layers and interstices. Specifically, I examine the intersections and interstices among life (body and population), power (technologies of power), and talent (human qualities and population) as the objects and objectives of education and state governance. Simply put, I interrogate talent as an apparatus of biopower to see how life is implicated in power and how power is modified by the introduction of life into its terrain and preoccupations (Genel, 2006).

Meanwhile, China's making and governing of educational subjects as talent is largely an imprint of Confucian culture, expressed, say, in President Xi's re-invocation of Confucian texts in his talent elaborations. Thus, I also compare China's talent making and governing with its Confucian prototype on their varied definitions of, and interpellations among, life (body and population), power (technologies of power), and talent (human qualities or population). In so doing, I hope not to reduce China's talent governmentality solely to the Foucauldian framework, but to map out the nuanced complexities of cultural context in ordering the way life, power, and talent get entangled in modern China's education-governance dynamics. To clarify, I am drawing upon both Foucault's biopower and Confucian thinking on two levels and for a more justified understanding of China's talent making and governing at the intersection of education and governance, not using one as a framework to gauge the other. On the one level, Foucault's biopower explicates the varying mechanisms and technologies entailed in classifying, selecting, and regulating talent as an object/objective at the intersections and interstices of sovereign power and biopower. On the other level, Confucian narratives historicize China's talent appeal to render visible some possible transformations in defining 'human', 'talent', and their interpellation, further clarifying the CCP's governing strategies in making educational subjects as talent.

Talent making and governing with China's new 'state governance' paradigm

As Genel (2006, p. 44) rightly observes, 'insofar as it functions through technologies of power, biopower must be analyzed in the concrete operations of its most localized procedures as well as in the manner in which it integrates itself into the more general processes of sovereignty and the law'. Bearing this caution in mind, I scrutinize two state talent policies, *Furthering Talent*

Work Decision (2003 by the Hu administration) and *Deepening Talent Development System and Mechanism Reform Suggestions* (2016 by the Xi administration), relevant public discourses on these policies, as well as some national 'talent-introduction' schemes. Albeit far from exhaustive, these texts provide an adequate lens for me to interrogate the education-governance interpellation of talent, life, and power as below.

'Everyone can become talent' as the trope of making talent into new kinds of people

The CPC claims that 'everyone *can become* talent' (2016, italics added), a statement I argue to be a political trope in China's talent making and governing. A rigorous discourse analysis explicates three characteristics of this talent-making logic. First, the notion 'talent' (*rencai*) is flattening out its semantic meaning into an empty signifier, an ordering principle, a label which makes (up) new kinds of people. Hacking's 'dynamic nominalism' (1986) is helpful here to clarify the function of talent as a label which, in marking certain people as talent, creates new and distinct kinds of people. Labels are never only mundane and procedural discursive categories; they make (up) reality in a way 'never neutral, objective, and automated' (Selwyn, 2015, p. 6). China's newly created talent population is subdivided into domestic/international talent, party cadre talent, entrepreneur talent, talent with special expertise, top-notch skilled talent, expatriate talent .... Here, talent is no longer merely a linguistic term signifying a quality or people with special expertise but an apparatus of intervention that differentiates and acts upon individuals.

Second, the function of talent as an ordering principle is inevitably entangled with an inclusion and exclusion trope. Specifically, to maintain its functionality as a classifying apparatus, talent must distinguish a small number of talented people from the majority not-talented people to ensure the former's symbolic-economic value against the excluded latter. Yet, paradoxically, more people need to be included in this talent pool to legitimize the state-proffered trope of 'everyone can become talent' and the ambition of building China into a 'largely talent-populated nation from a largely-populated nation'. Accordingly, the talent-not-talent boundary is to be continuously (re)drawn, because once the boundary is fixed, some are included whereas others excluded once for all. To liquidize the boundary, the making of kinds of people continuously evolves on different layers and dimensions, emplacing everyone on the pendulum of becoming and not-becoming talent.

Third, the trope 'everyone can become talent' changes 'the space of possibilities for personhood' (Hacking, 1986, p. 165). That is, people who do not count as talent today will become talent tomorrow, or vice versa. Furthermore, people's talent quality increases or decreases temporarily, or some people have more talent quality than others. That is, talent not just categorically divides people by kinds, but also differentiates people in degrees. For example, the population of scholar-talent can be further subdivided into high-level and top-notch talent, expatriate talent, youth talent, senior talent, experts, *changjiang* scholars, and youth *changjiang* scholars. This ordering by degree notably stretches the space of talent possibility by variables of gender, age, working experience, projects/publications, and potentiality.

With these three characteristics, we can say talent functions as an intervention apparatus and along a difference/differentiation logic. For talent to maintain its function as an ordering principle, people first need to be differentiated into groups in kind (with or without talent-quality) or in degree (with various amount of talent-quality) before they can be ordered and governed through difference (Lewis, 2018). Now let's unpack how this talent making is gradually and materially governed through a multiplicity of organizations, operations, and forces in modern China.

'Everyone can fully realize talent' as the dream to grid talent-governing mechanisms

As Li and Lowe (2016) rightly observe, universities in all nation-states inevitably partake in the global talent war as an effect of educational neoliberalization, linkage of knowledge economy and national economic survival, and universities' key role in producing knowledge. China's universities have thrust into this war for both domestic and overseas talent to an extent hardly comparable in other nation-states. Using university 'talent' recruitment programs as an example, this section untangles China's talent governing within its 'state governance' paradigm by the following questions: What apparatuses of power are entailed in the talent governmentality? How are they assembled under the CPC's sovereign power? How do talent and non-talent scholars self-govern themselves along with the state manipulation of talent as a form of bio-power?

Two features are noteworthy. First, among an ensemble of power institutions, CPC directly oversees China's talent development system through the Central Talent Work Coordination Team founded in 2003, which is commissioned to take full charge of China's talent-related strategic planning, policy study, macro-level guidance and mediation among varying institutions. Led by the Organization Department of the Central Committee of the CPC, this central coordination team has its members from twenty state institutions, forming an all-penetrating governing network. It is important to note that CPC's authoritative power is fully guaranteed through its structural articulations, both vertical and horizontal, of its party units across China, including schools. Thus, even though President Xi (2009) claims the CPC's leadership has 'shifted' from one of 'taking on everything' to 'mainly exercising political, ideological, and organizational leadership' under the 'state governance' structure (cited in Heath, 2016, p. 5), the CPC still undoubtedly assumes an authoritarian sovereign power in its state governing, including the governing of talent. Henceforth, it can be argued that China's talent biopolitics is distinct from Foucault's unpacking of the biopolitics dynamics in Western societies. In the latter, biopower is bound up with and yet remains distinct from the old sovereign power to the extent that power can be discerned at the interstices where it had otherwise remained undetected, whereas in the former, biopower is still largely subjugated to the sovereign power.

Second, in alignment with the CPC's centralized sovereign structure, multi-layered state-sponsored university talent recruitment plans constitute a comprehensive governing grid and space targeted at all types of academic talent trained domestically-internationally in a gesture of inclusion. With such a comprehensive space, 'everyone can fully realize his/her talent'. For example, the Chinese state launched the highest state-level program for attracting senior overseas talent in 2008, amended it in 2011 with one for junior overseas talent, and another one in 2012 for domestic talent. Meanwhile, since the 2000s, China's Ministry of Education has enacted various lower-level schemes for identifying-awarding domestic talent and introducing-including overseas talent who are possibly excluded from the state-level programs. Below is a juxtaposition of some of these mutually-supplementing talent programs which forms a multi-layered comprehensive talent making-governing network, further intersected with mirroring lower-level provincial and municipal network of talent schemes.

China's representative multi-layered talent schemes

Scheme	Year	Sponsors & targeted talent
Thousand Talent	2008	Central Talent Work Coordination Team (CTWCT), 2000 Overseas Top-Notch Science Talent (Associate/ Full Professors)
Youth Thousand Talent	2011	CTWCT, 400 overseas young scholars/scientists annually
Ten Thousand Talent	2012	National Top-Notch Talent Support Scheme, Central Organization, ten thousand domestic talent within ten years
Changjiang Scholar	1998 2011	Ministry of Education (MOE) & Hong Kong Li Ka Shing Foundation, 1st-Tier High-Level Talent Scheme, award-introduce domestic-overseas talent
Youth *Changjiang* Scholar	2015	MOE, award-introduce annually 200 young domestic-overseas scholars
New Century Excellent Talent	2004	MOE, 2nd-Tier Talent Scheme, award domestic young scholars (1000 annually)

Foucault's (1984) argument, biopower functions through a 'technology of population', through both individualizing and normalizing apparatuses, is helpful here to analyse the above talent mechanism of biopower. While the state set the norms of what and who counts as talent, these norms induce potential individual applicants to visualize and self-govern their talent potentiality toward the set norms. The individuals, the talent population, the nation state, education, and state governance are all worked toward the imperative objective and object of talent in a way that individuals' specific 'talent-quality' is inscribed within the intersected problem of education and state governance. For more people to be included in the talent pool, boundaries need to be (re)drawn by such variables as expertise areas, geographic domains, intellectual background, place of training (overseas and national), age (senior and youth), and nationality.

Among these varying apparatuses of intervention, 'age' is particularly significant in endowing talent with a temporality dimension, further stratifying talent into something already gained-exhibited and something to be potentially gained-exhibited. Dividing intellectual talent into 'associate and full professors' and 'young scholars' presumes that it takes time to develop, gain, and materialize 'talent-quality' and the former would usually have more credentials to showcase their 'talent-quality' than the latter. This temporality also justifies CPC's trope that 'everyone can fully realize his/her talent'. However, it is more of an intellectual 'time' than a biological one in that intellectuals' future performances are largely predicated upon referencing and improving their past performances, regardless of their biological age. That is, 'the past, present and future are each understood dynamically and in relation to one another' (Lewis, 2018, 690) with one temporality impacting another, liquidizing talent as something that can, and needs to, be developed, tested, and measured through some social administering mechanism.

These talent programs have since not only attracted a huge number of expatriate scholars to return to China (mostly eastern cities) but also incurred an unhealthy job-hopping wave among domestic scholars leaving the West for East China cities (see, Liu & Ha, 2016). The talent war has basically drained the intellectual reservoir in China's western universities to such an extent that the Ministry of Education (2014) has released several decrees to forbid abnormal talent auction among China's regional universities. The talent schemes apparently value overseas-obtained academic credentials more than domestically obtained ones (for example using SSCI journal publications to evaluate scholars' talent-quality), henceforth engendering an epidemic complaint and even resistance among the majority 'non-talent' domestic scholars against returning expatriate scholars or even fresh PhD graduates from renown overseas universities. A survey of young overseas-returning scholars in China's 6 universities show that they are less happy than expected in adapting themselves to the competitive academic and living environment (Li et al., 2015). It can be argued China's talent war in the past decade has complicated the power struggle among scholars, talent or not, largely disrupting the academic ecology in China's higher education (Nandu guancha blog post, 2019).

'Talent is most expensive in 21st century' as the logic of ordering life, power, and talent

'Talent (*rencai*) will become the most expensive thing in the 21st century', a joking punch line from the Chinese film *A World Without Thieves* (1997), becomes a well-accepted reality today. Namely, talent, or its constituents of 'capacity, competence, knowledge, skills', is economically valuable and 'needs to be trained, cultivated, channelled, regulated, and governed in alignment with the marketing economy so that it can circulate freely by the regulation of the market' (CPC, 2003, 2016). This economic value distinguishes talent from other types of life dispositions and qualities like honesty and intelligence, making the talent population a highly desirable commodity. In what way does the economic logic order China's talent making-governing at the intersection of education and state governance? How are human and talent as life dispositions and qualities (*cai*) interpellated, ordered, and regulated in a way to further act on the making (up) of educational subjects? Reading discourses as styles of reasoning further explicates three features of China's talent biopower administering as below.

First, talent becomes a new target for technologies of administration through infrastructures of statistics and 'datafication' (Lingard et al., 2013). Specifically, 'talent-people' need to be identified and singled out among the otherwise laymen through self-/other-nominations and by filling out various forms as a mechanism to transfer 'talent-quality' into displayable, articulable, and quantifiable numbers and figures. Such accountability and datafication, as Lingard et al. (2013, p. 552) rightly observe, constitutes 'a single commensurate space or surface for measure'. This information is then put online as a virtual panopticon-like governance apparatus for the public to incessantly check, evaluate, and critique, thus placing the potential 'talent-people' under public surveillance. Only in this way is the functionality of talent justified as a special life disposition/quality/capacity possessed by a very small number of people, and yet statistically/scientifically administered.

Second, the commercialization of 'talent-qualities' of skills and competencies transfigures 'talent-people' into a merchandise or a resource, which, just like other material objects, wait on the production line to be called and relayed to other posts. That is, the human subjectivity underpinning talent is subdued into an object or objective constituent in the line of production, circulation, and consumption. As a commodity, the economic value needs to be gauged through the capitalist investment-profit logic or what Jones (2013) calls 'market fundamentalism'. For example, when one sells his/her intellectual 'talent-quality', the buyer would expect some profit return in terms of publications, theories, or transferable knowledge and skills. The promised return would be further appraised by varying apparatuses of the state, market, organizations, and peers, all constituting a 'scientific, socialized and marketized talent evaluation system' (CPC, 2016). Thus, talent becomes not merely a material form but a site of power exercise where the value of talent is determined-appraised through an ensemble of surveillance mechanisms.

Lastly, what is intriguing about talent as a type of merchandise is its liquidity and limitrophy, in that what guarantees its value is mostly its potentiality, presumed to be tapped and transformed into other forms of valuable product. Nevertheless, the present talent value is gauged and affirmed by one's past achievements. It is the potential value of talent, anticipated but not guaranteed, that is priced in the talent auction market. Underpinning this rationale is a linear development logic turning talent into a resource to be cultivated and transposed to the production line. To borrow Lewis's (2018) theorization, the (self)-governing of talent works along a potential logic, namely, 'to work on the self in the present based on knowledge about the past, in order to achieve a more desirable future' (685).

So far, this paper analyses China's talent making and governing at the intersection of education and state governance, explicating the ways in which talent functions as an apparatus of power, an ordering principle, and an intervention mechanism in rejoining life (human persons and population), state governance, marketing economy, and education. What strikes out is the neoliberal 'market fundamentalism' as the dominant governing logic by which the value of talent is determined, and China's high staking of talent development in empowering its national-global competitiveness. As CPC (2016) claims, China's talent reform is to 'turn the advantage of talent as *human capital* to that of knowledge, science and technology, and industry, vitalizing all the force of labour, knowledge, skills, management, and capital such that all the springs of sources potentially conducive to the production of social wealth are in full flow' (italics mine).

Please note talent is here explicitly and officially defined as 'human capital'. The above analysis also affirms that China's intended meaning of talent as a gloss of '*rencai*' echoes the saying of the English term 'human capital', namely, 'the stock of knowledge, habits, social and personality attributes, including activity, embodied in the ability to perform labour so as to produce economic value' (Goldin, 2016). Then, why do the Chinese prefer talent over 'human capital', a term more commonly used in Western societies? Why does President Xi persistently re-invoke Confucian '*rencai*' (talent) discourses in elaborating on modern talent, education, and state governance? I argued at the beginning of this paper that China's strategic appeal to talent making-governing at the juncture of education and state governance is more an imprint of Confucian educational culture than a mere neoliberalization effect of education. Comparison of China's talent making-governing dynamics to its Confucian prototype is thus needed to articulate possible transformations regarding their definitions of 'human', 'talent', and human-talent interpellation.

Comparing 'talent' making and governing with Confucian thought

Literally called 'teaching-as-transforming' (*jiaohua*), Confucian education interlocks with state governing to the extent that the sovereign-subject relationship is configured along a teaching-learning dynamic, with Confucian literati populating the state-governing structure as official-scholars (Han, 2013). With a salient moral purpose (Di & McEwan, 2016), Confucian learning as a form of dao-learning aims to cultivate a person into an exemplary person (*junzi*) with both 'virtue' (*de*) and 'talent-capabilities' (*cai*), called *xiancai* (literally, virtue-talent). Put succinctly, the Confucian culture foregrounds education as a political tool of state governance, cultivating official-scholars with both virtue and talent (Zhao 2017b, 2019). In a word, the Confucian prototype of talent further accents both virtuous dispositions and talent-capabilities as expressed in the Chinese term of *decai jianbei*.

When talking about *'rencai'* (literally, human-talent, the original Chinese term glossed as talent), modern Chinese people indeed resort to this Confucian term of *'decai jianbei'* as a more specific articulation of what counts as an all-rounded 'talent-person'. Chinese education as an imprint of Confucian educational heritage has always intended to train and make such all-rounded talent-persons. When meeting with teachers and students in Beijing Normal University, President Xi (2014) re-asserted that education is to make talent, entailing both 'nurturing humans (*ren*) and nurturing talent-capabilities (*cai*)' with the former being the root of education. The root of human-nurturing is to teach students to establish themselves with 'moral excellences (*de*) because humans without moral excellence can't establish themselves'. In elucidating how *cai* (talent-capability) and *de* (moral excellence) define and relate to each other in establishing a human being, President Xi re-invokes a statement by Sima Guang (1019-1086), a Northern Song Neo-Confucian official-scholar and historian-politician who spent 19 years to compile the first colossal chronicles of Chinese history (*Zizhi Tongjian*), a *magnum opus* on Confucian ritual-governance as well as a must-read for imperial sovereignties.

The statement President Xi (2014) re-invokes, 'talent-capability (*cai*) is what supplements virtue (*de*) whereas virtue (*de*) is what founds talent-capability (*cai*)', was Sima's commentary on the decadence and demise of the Zhou dynasty (1046-256 BCE). The historian-politician Sima differentiates 'talent-capability' from 'virtue', which laymen often conflate in the notion of *'xian'*. The last Zhou dynasty emperor prioritized 'talent-capability' over 'virtue', an ideology that Sima claims directly resulted in the demise of the Zhou dynasty. Sima illustrates this *de-cai* ordering with an example of bamboo and gold: 'The bamboo from Yunmei is famous for its hardness, yet without tempering it and adding some features, it cannot penetrate into the hardness; the gold from Tangxi is famous for its sharpness, yet without melting and beating, it cannot be used to hit the strong'. What is noteworthy here is Sima's nuanced differentiation between *'de'* and *'cai'*, with the former naming virtuous excellences such as upright, straight, middle ground, and harmony, and the latter human qualities such as smartness, perceptiveness, strength, and solidness. While the former are qualities more needed when a person deals with other beings, the latter is more related to attitude when coping with things.

Interestingly, when *'de'* and *'cai'* are re-invoked today, they take up new nuances and textures. For example, in his talk at the National Party School Working Meeting, President Xi (2015) redefines a party member's *'de'* (virtue) as his/her *'dangxing'* (party-nature/loyalty), something cultivated only through rigorously studying the party constitution, regulations, and rules. Similarly, current talent cultivation serves primarily to enhance people's learning competencies, practicability, and innovation (CPC, 2016).

This brief comparison finds that although President Xi repeatedly reinvokes Confucian talent discourses in his talent elaboration at the intersection of education and state governance, these two forms of talent appeal, expressed respectively as *xiancai* and *rencai*, differ in their form, configuration, structure, and function. While Confucian education accents making a person into an exemplary one who can establish oneself with moral excellence, today's talent, partly as an effect of the neoliberalization of education, is more about gaining skills and capabilities transferrable into economic value, subordinating the subject's virtuous dispositions. Accordingly, talent turns into a merchandise ordered by its use value and economic potential, as is best expressed in President Xi's adaptation of Mencius' statement 'getting the good person in the world to share one's expertise as a joy' into an instrumental strategy of 'convening talent from all over the world for [China's] use'. Seen this way, the current term *rencai* (human-talent), even though resonating well with the Confucian notion *xiancai* (virtue-talent), is semantically more akin to the English term 'human capital'. It can thus be argued that China's appeal to 'talent' discourse as a global and culturally re-invoked notion, as well as its re-conceptualization of it as something no longer natural but cultivable through education, is a political strategy rather than an authentic cultural renaissance gesture.

Conclusion

This paper employs Foucault's biopower hypothesis to examine modern China's talent making and governing at the intersection of education and state governance and against the Confucian talent prototype. While this issue of talent differs from the Western problem of sickness and health in Foucault's unpacking of noso-politics, 'talent' can indeed be viewed as a form of biopower, not only making (up) new kinds of people but also normalizing a certain population as the objective/object of state governance in a way resonating with and yet not reducible to the Confucian prototype. The working logic of this biopower of talent bespeaks three features. First, the trope that 'everyone can become talent' reconfigures talent as an ordering principle which classifies people into types of possessing or not possessing talent-quality and groups with different amount of talent-quality. Second, the dream that 'everyone can realize talent' is materialized through an ensemble of governing apparatuses along an inclusion and exclusion logic. Finally, an economic logic that 'talent is the most expensive thing in the 21st century' underpins the talent making and governing dynamics as an effect of global neoliberalization of education. Compared to the Confucian human-talent interpellation which foregrounds both virtuous dispositions and talent-capabilities, China's contemporary talent-making is more focused on the cultivation of knowledge, skills, and competencies that can empower the 21st-century educational subjects into more competitive human resources, hoping to turn China from 'a largely-populated nation to a largely talent-populated nation' (CPC 2003).

Disclosure statement

No potential conflict of interest was reported by the author.

ORCID

Weili Zhao http://orcid.org/0000-0002-0552-9347

References

Bryce, T., Nellis, M., Corrigan, A., Gallagher, H., Lee, P., & Sercombe, H. (2010). Biometric surveillance in schools: Cause for concern or case for curriculum? *Scottish Educational Review*, *42*(1), 3–22.

Chinese Communist Party Central Committee. (2016). Guanyu shenhua rencai fazhan jizhi tizhi gaige de yijian. Retrieved from http://www.xinhuanet.com/politics/2016-03/21/c_1118398308.htm

Chinese Communist Party Central Committee and State Council (2003). Zhongguo zhongyang guowuyuan guanyu jinyibu jiaqiang rencai gongzuo de jueding. Retrieved from http://www.gov.cn/test/2005-07/01/content_11547.htm

Di, X., & McEwan, H. (Eds.). (2016). *Chinese philosophy on teaching and learning: Xueji (學記) In the twenty-first century*. Albany: State University of New York Press.

Feng, B. (2014). Xhili linian cong guanli dao zhili: Dangdai zhongguo shehui jianshe linian de shenghua. http://www.qunzh.com/ldjs/sh/shzl/201412/t20141225_5298.html

Foucault, M. (1977). *Discipline and punish: The Birth of the prison*. London: Allen Lane.

Foucault, M. (1978). The history of sexuality. *Vol. 1: An introduction*. Harmondsworth: Penguin.

Foucault, M. (1984). The politics of health in the eighteenth century. In P. Rainbow (Ed.), *The Foucault reader* (pp. 273–289). New York (NY): Vintage Books.

Foucault, M. (2007). *Security, territory, population. Lectures at the Collège De France*, 1977–1978. Basingstoke: Palgrave Macmillan.

Genel, K. (2006). The question of biopower: Foucault and Agamben. *Rethinking Marxism*, *18*(1), 43–62. doi:10.1080/08935690500410635

Goldin, C. (2016). Human capital. *Handbook of cliometrics*, 55–86.

Gong, T., Collins, P., & Chan, H. S. (2017). The quality of governance in China and beyond: Introduction to special issue. *Public Administration and Development*, *37*(3), 155–159. doi:10.1002/pad.1802

Hacking, I. (1986). Making Up People. In T. L. Heller, M. Sosna, and D. E. Wellbery (Eds). *Reconstructing individualism: Autonomy, individuality, and the self in western thought* (pp. 161–171). Stanford, CA: Stanford University Press.

Han, S. (2013). Confucian states and learning life: Making scholar-officials and social learning a political contestation. *Comparative Education*, *49*(1), 57–71. doi:10.1080/03050068.2012.740220

Heath, T. R. (2016). *China's new governing party paradigm: Political renewal and the pursuit of national rejuvenation*. New York (NY): Routledge.

Hope, A. (2005). Panopticism, play and the resistance of surveillance: Case studies of the observation of student Internet use in UK schools. *The British Journal of Sociology of Education*, *26*(3), 359–373.

Hope, A. (2009). CCTV, school surveillance and social control. *British Educational Research Journal, 35*(6), 891–907. doi:10.1080/01411920902834233

Hope, A. (2016). Biopower and school surveillance technologies 2.0. *British Journal of Sociology of Education, 37*(7), 885–904. doi:10.1080/01425692.2014.1001060

Hu, J, (2012). Zai zhongguo gongchandang dishibaci quanguo daibiao dahui shangde baogao. Retrieved from http://news.china.com.cn/politics/2012/11/20/content_27165856.htm

Jones, G. (2013). Afterword: Rates of exchange: Neoliberalism and the value of higher education. *International Studies in Sociology of Education, 23*(3), 273–280. doi:10.1080/09620214.2013.844943

Kuehn, L. (2008). Surveillance 2.0: The "Information Panopticon" and Education. *Our Schools, Our Selves, 2008*, 81–91.

Lewis, S. (2018). PISA 'Yet To Come': governing schooling through time, difference and potential. *British Journal of Sociology of Education, 39*(5), 683–697. doi:10.1080/01425692.2017.1406338

Li, T., Cheng, L., & Fang, S. (2015). Gaoxiao haigui qingnian jiaoshi shengcun xianzhuang fenxi. *Xuehai, 6*, 210–216.

Li, Z., & Lowe, J. (2016). Mobile student to mobile worker: The role of universities in the 'war for talent. *British Journal of Sociology of Education, 37*(1), 11–29. doi:10.1080/01425692.2015.1095636

Lingard, B., Martino, W., & Rezai-Rashti, G. (2013). Testing regimes, accountabilities and education policy: Commensurate global and national developments. *Journal of Education Policy, 28*(5), 539–556. doi:10.1080/02680939.2013.820042

Liu, J., & Ha, M. (2016). Yidai yilu beijingxia zhongguo dongxibu gaoxiao jiaoshi liudong de guaidian yanjiu. *Chongqing Higher Education Research, 4*(5), 20–25.

Mills, C. (2013). Biopoltical Life. In J. Nilsson and S. Wallenstein (Eds). *M. Foucault, Biopoltics and Governmentality* (pp. 73–90). Huddinge: Sodertorn University.

Ministry of Education. (2014). Jinzhi dongbu gaoxiao fu zhongxibu gaoxiao wa rencai. Retrieved from http://news.sina.com.cn/c/2014-01-01/224529137506.shtml

Nandu, G. (2019). Zhongguo gaoxiao rencai de liudong keneng buzhishi weile qian [Blog post]. Retrieved from https://www.jiemodui.com/Item/105431.html?ft=detail&fid=94750

Popkewitz, T. S. (2007). *Cosmopolitanism and the age of school reform: Science,education, and making society by making the child.* New York (NY): Routledge.

Rabinow, P., & Rose, N. (2006). Biopower today. *BioSocieties, 1*(2), 195–217. doi:10.1017/S1745855206040014

Roxburgh, H. (2017). Winning the war for talent in China. Retrieved from http://hrmagazine.co.uk/article-details/winning-the-war-for-talent-in-china

Selwyn, N. (2015). Data entry: Towards the critical study of digital data and education. *Learning, Media and Technology, 40*(1), 64–82. doi:10.1080/17439884.2014.921628

Sima, G. (1019-1086). *Zizhi tongjian·zhouji·zhouji yi.* Retrieved from http://www.gushice.com/bookview_450.html

Stromseth, J. R., Malesky, E. J., & Gueorguiev, D. D. (2017). *China's governance puzzle: Enabling transparency and participation in a single-party state.* Cambridge: Cambridge University Press.

Taylor, E. (2014). *Surveillance schools: Security, discipline and control in contemporary Education.* Basingstoke: Palgrave Macmillan.

Wang, H., & Miao, L. (2018). *Rencai zhanzheng 2.0.* Beijing: Dongfang Press.

Xi, J. (2009). Guanyu xinzhongguo liushinian dangde jianshe de jidian sikao. *Xuexi Shibao: Study Times.* Retrieved from http://theory.people.com.cn/GB/10129311.html

Xi, J. (2013). Xijinping chuxi quanguo zuzhigongzuo huiyi bing fabiao zhongyao jianghua. Retrieved from http://www.gov.cn/jrzg/2013-06/29/content_2437072.htm

Xi, J. (2014). Xi jinping tong Beijing shifan daxue shisheng daibiao zuotanshi de jianghua. Retrieved from http://www.chinanews.com/gn/2014/09-10/6575002.shtml

Xi, J. (2015). Zai quanguo dangxiao gongzuo huiyi shangde jianghua. Retrieved from http://www.xinhuanet.com/politics/2016-05/01/c_128951529.htm

Xi, J. (2016). Zai qingzhu zhongguo gongchandang chengli jiushiwu zhounian dahui shangde jianghua. Retrieved from http://www.xinhuanet.com/politics/2016-07/01/c_1119150660.htm

Xi, J. (2018). Zai zhongguo kexueyuan dishijiuci yuanshidahui, zhongguo gongchengyuan dishisici yuanshidahui shangde jianghua. Retrieved from http://www.xinhuanet.com/politics/2018-05/28/c_1122901308.htm

Zhao, W. (2017a). "Observation" as China's civic education pedagogy: A historical perspective and a dialogue with Michel Foucault. Discourse: Studies in the Cultural Politics of Education. doi:10.1080/01596306.2017.1404444

Zhao, W. (2017b). Re-invigorating the being of language in international education: Unpacking Confucius' "wind-pedagogy" in Yijing as an exemplar. Discourse: Studies in the Cultural Politics of Education. doi:10.1080/01596306.2017.1354286

Zhao, W. (2019). China's education, curriculum knowledge and cultural inscriptions: Dancing with the wind. New York and London: Routledge.

Talents and distributive justice: An interview with Hillel Steiner

Mitja Sardoč

Hillel Steiner is Emeritus Professor of Political Philosophy and Honorary Research Fellow at the University of Manchester, and a Fellow of the British Academy. He is also Research Professor in Philosophy and in the Center for the Philosophy of Freedom at the University of Arizona. A Canadian, he was born and grew up in Toronto, and studied economics as an undergraduate at the University of Toronto, where he became actively involved in socialist politics and the American civil rights movement. His move into political philosophy occurred in the course of his doctoral research at the University of Manchester and was partly due to his encountering the philosophical methods of conceptual analysis.

An adequate account of justice, he came to believe, must be one derived from points of conceptual intersection between moral philosophy, jurisprudence and economic theory. This project eventually issued in his prize-winning monograph, *An Essay on Rights* (Blackwell 1994; revised edition, Oxford University Press, forthcoming), where he develops what has come to be called a *left libertarian* theory of distributive justice – in his case, a theory that is derived from analyses of negative liberty, rights, moral pluralism and economic rationality. The distinctive foundational core of that theory is its close focus on the conditions necessary and sufficient for all the rights in a set of rights to be *compossible*: that is, for all the duties correlatively entailed by those rights to be jointly performable.

Steiner's papers have appeared in journals of philosophy, economics, law and political science, and many have been reprinted in edited collections within those disciplines. He is also co-author (with Matthew Kramer and Nigel Simmonds) of *A Debate Over Rights: Philosophical Enquiries* (Oxford University Press 1998); co-editor (with Geraint Parry) of *Freedom and Trade*, three volumes (Routledge 1998); co-editor (with Peter Vallentyne) of *The Origins of Left-Libertarianism: An Anthology of Historical Writings*, and *Left-Libertarianism and Its Critics: The Contemporary Debate* (Palgrave Macmillan 2000); and co-editor (with Ian Carter and Matthew Kramer) of *Freedom: A Philosophical Anthology* (Blackwell 2007). His current research projects are focused on exploitation and the concept of 'the just price', and on the application of libertarian principles to global and genetic inequalities.

Mitja Sardoč (PhD) is senior research associate at the Educational Research Institute in Ljubljana (Slovenia) where he is member of the 'Social Contract in the 21st Century' research programme. He is author of scholarly articles and editor of a number of journal special issues on citizenship education, multiculturalism, toleration, equality of opportunity and patriotism. He is Managing Editor of *Theory and Research in Education* [http://tre.sagepub.com/] and Editor-in-Chief of *The Handbook of Patriotism* [http://refworks.springer.com/ Patriotism] to be published by Springer.

For much of its history, the notion of talent has been associated with the idea of 'careers open to talent'. Its emancipatory promise of upward social mobility has ultimately radically transformed the distribution of advantaged social positions and has had a lasting influence on the very idea of social status itself. What is your view on the emancipatory promise of talents?

HS: The starting-point for any coherent normative thinking about talents has to be the fact that *talents are labour products*: their creation and development requires the application of gestational, nutritional, medical, educational and training services. I fully agree that the idea of 'careers open to talent' has the emancipatory promise you mention. But to fulfill that promise, it is vital that this emancipation be *universal* in its incidence. If acquiring an advantaged social position is to be the result of talent rather than luck or inherited privilege, then presumably the same applies to the acquisition of the means to produce that talent. When it comes to the criterion for assigning social positions, there's not much emancipatory promise in replacing one arbitrarily distributed factor with another arbitrarily distributed factor.

Besides its inextricable link with equality of opportunity, the notion of talent came to be associated also with some of the most pressing contemporary issues as diverse as the 'war for talent', brain drain, immigration policies, talent management, global meritocracy, the 'excellence gap', the 'ownership' of natural resources, ability taxation etc. Why has the notion of talent come to figure as some sort of 'buzzword' in these discussions?

HS: It's that link with equality of opportunity that lies at the core of the explanation for talent's centrality in all these issues. Equality of opportunity is commonly and correctly associated with the idea of a 'level playing-field'. One requirement for a level playing-field is the absence of barriers that favour some players over others. National borders constitute such barriers just as much as do racism and sexism. And the same is true with regard to unequal access to the resources needed for talent production. Players whose access to the aforesaid services is inferior to that of others will generally perform less well than those others. Athletes competing in the same running race do not start at different times or from different starting-lines or, for that matter, from different levels of ingested performance-enhancing drugs. And if they did, we would not regard their comparative finishing positions as due to their talent.

Unlike concepts traditionally associated with distributive justice, e.g. fairness, (in)equality, desert, equality of opportunity as well as justice itself, the notion of talent has received only limited examination. Why you think the idea of talent has been at the fringes of scholarly interest?

HS: A major reason, I think, is that persons' talents are often and unreflectively assumed to be basically natural or fixed personal characteristics, rather than products of choices. What's true, of course, is that one of the major factors entering into the production of talents – namely, the quality of persons' genetic endowments – has long been unchosen, a matter of unavoidable brute luck (though, as scholarly interest has recently begun to reflect, this will increasingly cease to be true with the gradual advance of gene-editing techniques). What has never been true, however, is that the quality of the other factors entering into the production of persons' talents is unchosen. These post-conception factor inputs are very much objects of choice: choices made by parents, by politicians and, upon their attainment of adulthood, by those persons themselves.

The 'standard' egalitarian conception of distributive justice views talents as a form of unfair advantage. As you write in your paper 'Silver Spoons and Golden Genes: Talent Differentials and Distributive Justice', 'the egalitarian proviso on natural resource distribution requires that those who produce children with golden genetic endowments [...] owe net transfer payments to those who do not'. What would be the main shortcomings of this distributive arrangement?

HS: Conceptions of distributive justice that view talents as a form of unfair advantage are, I think, reflecting – not inaccurately – the socio-economic conditions under which talents have long been produced in most societies. It's simply beyond question that these conditions have consisted in vast inequalities of access to the aforementioned chosen factor inputs of talent production. But even if (or when) those inequalities are eliminated, there would still be – prior to the consummation of the gene-editing revolution – unavoidable inequalities between different persons' genetic endowments: there would still be persons with genetically driven disabilities and their genetically advantaged counterparts.

My transfer payment proposal would provide the parents of genetically disadvantaged children with additional resources to secure extra factor inputs – primarily medical, educational and pastoral services – to offset those disabilities, by developing whichever talents those children are capable of possessing: ideally, developing them to the level of talent equality at the threshold of adulthood, when their further development becomes a matter of choice for those persons themselves. And part of the reasoning for requiring these payments to come from 'those who produce children with golden genetic endowments' goes as follows: (1) insofar as children's genetic endowments are deliverances of nature; and (2) since justice requires an interpersonally equal distribution of (the value of all) natural resources; and (3) since parents with genetically advantaged children thereby enjoy a share of natural resource value that is, *ceteris paribus*, greater than do those with genetically disadvantaged children; therefore (4) the former owe the latter that equalizing payment. (A more fine-grained presentation of the profile and justification of this distributive arrangement – and one that takes account of the fact that *ceteris* are not invariably *paribus* – will appear in my forthcoming paper, 'Ancestors and Descendants'.)

I suppose that this distributive arrangement might be thought to have one main shortcoming: namely, that some parents of genetically advantaged children may be unable to afford the payment required of them. Against this objection I would argue, first, that other requirements of the wider theory of distributive justice in which this payment proposal is embedded (see my *An Essay on Rights*, 1994) entail everyone's entitlement to an unconditional basic income. Secondly, I guess we would all agree that persons considering procreating have a serious duty to ensure that they have sufficient resources – including insurance – to cover the costs they may thereby incur. Parents who can afford to cover those costs, but don't, are engaged in something akin to child abuse.

You have written extensively on the distribution of natural resources (including talents). How have you become interested in the idea of natural resources? What triggered your interest in this area of scholarly research?

HS: A clarification: talents are labour products; they are *not* natural resources. Indeed, it was partly that fact that first engaged my interest in the connection between talents and natural resources, in the 1980s. But long before then I was already deeply immersed – like so many others – in trying to identify the conditions under which the demands of equality can be consistently reconciled with those of individual liberty. And I found those conditions in the implications of the egalitarian proviso on natural resource distribution. The philosophical origin of that proviso lies in the 17th century work of John Locke, widely regarded as a founding figure in the theory of classical liberalism. Arguing against the prevalent absolutist doctrine of the *Divine Right of Kings* – that all persons are the property of their rulers – Locke maintained that each person is rightfully a self-owner: each person's body is, so to speak, owner-occupied, unlike the body of a slave. Consequently, each person is the rightful owner of the labour of that body and, hence, the rightful owner of that labour's products. But Locke recognized that some ownable things – namely, natural resources – are not the products of any person's labour, are therefore permissibly available for everyone's use and, moreover, are finite in their extent. So he included a proviso limiting the amount of natural resources that any one person could justly privatise: in appropriating natural resources, he said, each person must ensure that he or she leaves 'enough and as good' for others, or must compensate them for not doing so. Indeed, I've argued that, in the absence of some such proviso, the Lockean premise of self-ownership generates mutually contradictory implications.

Over the intervening centuries this proviso has been subject to several different interpretations, but I think the simplest and most coherent one is that it entitles each person to an equal share of natural resources or its value equivalent. In effect, owners of property with natural resources are to be taxed 100% of the *difference* between that property's gross market value and the value of any improvements made to it, and each person is entitled to an equal portion of that tax. This interpretation of the proviso has generated a family of distributive justice theories (of which mine is but one) that has come to be called *Left Libertarianism*. Such theories share classical liberalism's endorsement of private property and free markets, provided that everyone receives their justly equal share of natural resource value – paradigmatically, in the form of an unconditional basic income. To the extent that persons are deprived of that entitlement – to the extent that they are, morally speaking, *robbed* – they are vulnerable to unjust exploitation even in free markets and, more generally, the prevailing distribution of *legal* property rights must be seen as tainted with injustice.

As you rightly acknowledge in your paper 'Silver Spoons and Golden Genes: Talent Differentials and Distributive Justice', the concept of 'natural resources' is very complex. Do you find the idea of talents complex as well? Why/Why not?

HS: Yes, the idea of talents is indeed complex, but not unmanageably so – at least for purposes related to thinking about distributive justice. The complexity of the concept of natural resources is largely due to the diversity it comprehends. This includes not only all portions of the Earth's surface but also sub- and super-terranian resources such as oil, gold and uranium deposits, the electromagnetic spectrum, the ozone layer, air-space, terrains with benign climates and terrains with serious geological faults – and also, as I've suggested, vast quantities of genetic material. All of these things are used in the course of human activity: they are bought and sold and thus have ascertainable values which vary immensely in their magnitude.

Talents also have varying values and, apart from their considerable diversity, a further reason for their complexity is that cultural factors play a significant role in determining those variations. As Erasmus observed, 'In the land of the blind, the one-eyed man is king'. Disabilities are the obverse of talents and most societies develop commensurating standards for determining the *extent* to which qualitatively diverse disabilities are disabling: standards reflected, for example, in the awards of compensation in legal cases of personal injury. Presumably some of the evaluational complexity, posed by the cultural relativity and diversity of talents, can be similarly reduced by reference to compensation awards for losses of talent due to personal injury, illness, etc. And, of course, insofar as social factors like globalization and enhanced communication techniques have the effect of levelling playing-fields, they extend the scope of equal opportunity and reduce the complexity fostered by cultural differences.

What aspect of talents' nature do you find most important for discussions about distributive justice (and why), e.g. their moral arbitrariness, social desirability, unequal distribution, their non-transferability?

HS: I'm very tempted to say 'All of the above', but that's not quite correct. Talents are morally arbitrary only to the extent that their production factors are distributed in morally arbitrary – unjust – ways. In all other respects, talents – what they are and who has which ones of them – are things on the development of which persons deliberately choose to expend time, effort and considerable reflection. And that seems sufficient reason to exclude them from the category of being morally arbitrary. Why some talents are more socially desirable than others is a fascinating question, but probably one more competently answered by anthropologists, sociologists and psychologists, than by me.

It is talents' unequal distribution and their non-transferability that are most directly engaged by my work. Unlike other forms of wealth, 'human capital' (as talents are sometimes described) is, in one respect, non-transferable. I can transfer my computer, my money and my factory to you. In doing so, I relinquish possession of them and you acquire it. But there's a sense in which I can also transfer my philosophising skill to you: namely, by teaching you. The essential difference, of course, is that your acquiring possession of that skill does *not* entail my relinquishing it. This difference in transferability does indeed point to a much deeper philosophical issue – the uncertain ontological character of *information* – which, I think, underlies many practical policy debates around intellectual property rights, and with which philosophers are only beginning to grapple.

For my purposes, however, it's the *non*-transferable aspect of talents – the fact that I can refuse to teach you, and thereby retain that talent for my exclusive possession (just as I can retain my computer) – that matters. Teaching or, more broadly, imparting information is something that no one can justly be compelled to do: liberal values in general, and self-ownership in particular, obviously prohibit the enforced (uncontracted) performance of self-owned labour. So if, as I've suggested, children are justly entitled to an equal share of the factors of talent production, the services providing those transferable factors have to be voluntarily supplied, through exchange or donation.

The idea of moral arbitrariness plays a central role in discarding talents as a form of unfair advantage in the process of competing for advantaged social positions. Is there a way to overcome this impasse?

HS: The way to overcome it is, as with any competition, to arrange things so as to ensure that the interpersonal distribution of advantaged social positions is purely a result of the competitors' own choices. And the only arrangement that can satisfy that requirement is one in which that result is not affected by any inequality in those competitors' initial starting positions. Starting positions are the crucial consideration for determining whether a social position has been secured by the exercise of talent. The talent of a large corporation's CEO is assessed *not* by reference to the current stock-market valuation of her corporation's shares, but rather by reference to the size of the *difference* between those shares' current valuation and their valuation at the time when she first became CEO. Much the same is true of any teacher, whose teaching talent is not accurately measured by the grades his students achieve, but rather by the difference between those grades and the ones they achieved before he became their teacher. *Value added* is the proper measure of talent, and the only way of identifying it requires reference to the value of players' initial conditions. For the outcome of social competition to be both fair and talent-tracking, those conditions must be ones of equal value.

Advocates of critical egalitarianism argue that individuals may not deserve the results of the 'lottery of birth' as they have equated talents [as a form of 'natural' inequality] with 'social' inequality. What, if anything, makes talents problematic from a distributive perspective?

HS: As I've suggested, those egalitarians are undoubtedly correct if their objection is a response to the longstanding vast inequalities of initial access to the factors of talent production. It's the current distribution of talents that is problematic. And it's problematic precisely because, with some notable exceptions, it tends to replicate those access inequalities over time and thereby to generate a distribution of advantaged social positions that widely diverges from the distribution that would prevail if that initial access were equal. The profiles of current and past distributions of advantaged social positions are clearly *not* isomorphic with the sort of standard used for assessing the talent of teachers and CEOs.

That said, I strongly disagree with those egalitarians whose objection further extends to unequal distributions of advantaged social positions *per se*. For although justice demands talent-equality at the threshold of adulthood, it does not require persons to exercise those talents once they have crossed that threshold. Some adults, perhaps many, may choose to exercise and further develop their own talents in pursuit of advantaged social positions. But if others choose to exempt themselves – partly or wholly – from participation in arenas of social competition, and thereby to forgo the advantaged social positions attendant upon that participation, then it's extremely unclear how egalitarians can find injustice in their doing so: one cannot violate one's own rights. Taxing those who choose to compete, in order to subsidise those who choose otherwise, simply amounts to the latter's exploitation of the former. What justice requires is that the distribution of advantaged social positions tracks choices made from equal starting-points.

One last question: is there any issue associated with distributive justice and talents (or natural resources in general) that contemporary discussions have either neglected or outrightly ignored?

HS: Contemporary philosophical discussions of distributive justice – and, for that matter, discussions in public policy circles too – have long acknowledged the importance of children receiving some measure of equal nutritional, medical and educational services. And these measures are well understood as having to be ones that take remedial account of at least some variations and inequalities in the background circumstances of different children. So I guess I have nothing novel to add to those discussions.

What I think is not yet receiving the level of attention that it warrants in these forums is indeed the issue of genetic inequalities. To be sure, there is now a slowly growing body of respectable philosophical literature on this subject, but it is still some considerable distance away from having attained anything like widespread familiarity. My impression is that at least part of the explanation for this relative inattention is an understandable aversion to venture anywhere near the intellectual terrain inhabited by the last century's eugenics movement and the horrendous political doctrines it was seen to foster. But, however understandable and even laudable its motivation is, that aversion is sorely misplaced. Genetic inequalities *do* exist: numerous disabling conditions, both physiological and psychological, are increasingly found to be ones to which their sufferers are *genetically* predisposed. No account of the relation between distributive justice and talent can be regarded as adequate if it glosses over this scientifically proven fact. There is an enormous difference between 'careers open to talent' and 'careers open to the genetically gifted'. Early 20th century eugenics failed to recognize this difference. We should not repeat that error.

Index

Note: Folios in **bold** indicate tables and with "n" indicates notes.